Performing/Guzzling

Kim Gordon

RIZZOLI
NEW YORK
New York · Paris · London · Milan

First published in the United States of America in 2009 by
Rizzoli International Publications, Inc.
300 Park Avenue South, New York, NY 10010
www.rizzoliusa.com

In collaboration with

Nieves
Ankerstrasse 20, 8004 Zurich, Switzerland
www.nievesbooks.com

Thanks to Kerry Schuss, Hilton Als, Coco Hayley Gordon Moore, Thurston Moore, Andrew Kesin, Jutta Koether, Bill Nace, Cody Ranaldo, Richard Prince, Amoreen Armetta, Christopher Luxtón, Henry Casey, Lauren Cecil, Phyllis Collazo, Jacob Lehman, Charles Miers, Ellen Nidy, Anthony Petrillose, and Rob Trostle. Special thanks to KS Art, New York.

Editors: Benjamin Sommerhalder and Julie Schumacher
Art Direction: Benjamin Sommerhalder
Design: Christopher Luxton
Production: Kaija Markoe

Work on pages 35 and 101 is based on *True Norwegian Black Metal* photographs by Peter Beste.
Work on the cover and pages 19, 60, 61, 86, 87, 89, 93, and 113 are used with permission by *The New York Times*.
Work on the cover and page 87 are used with permission by AP Images.
Work on page 18, 28, and 29 used with permission from *Daily Hampshire Gazette*.

Every attempt has been made to obtain appropriate permissions.
Any errors or omissions will be rectified in future editions or reprints.

Printed in China

2010 2011 2012 2013/ 10 9 8 7 6 5 4 3 2 1

ISBN-13: 978-0-8478-3341-2
Library of Congress Catalog Control Number: 2009922128

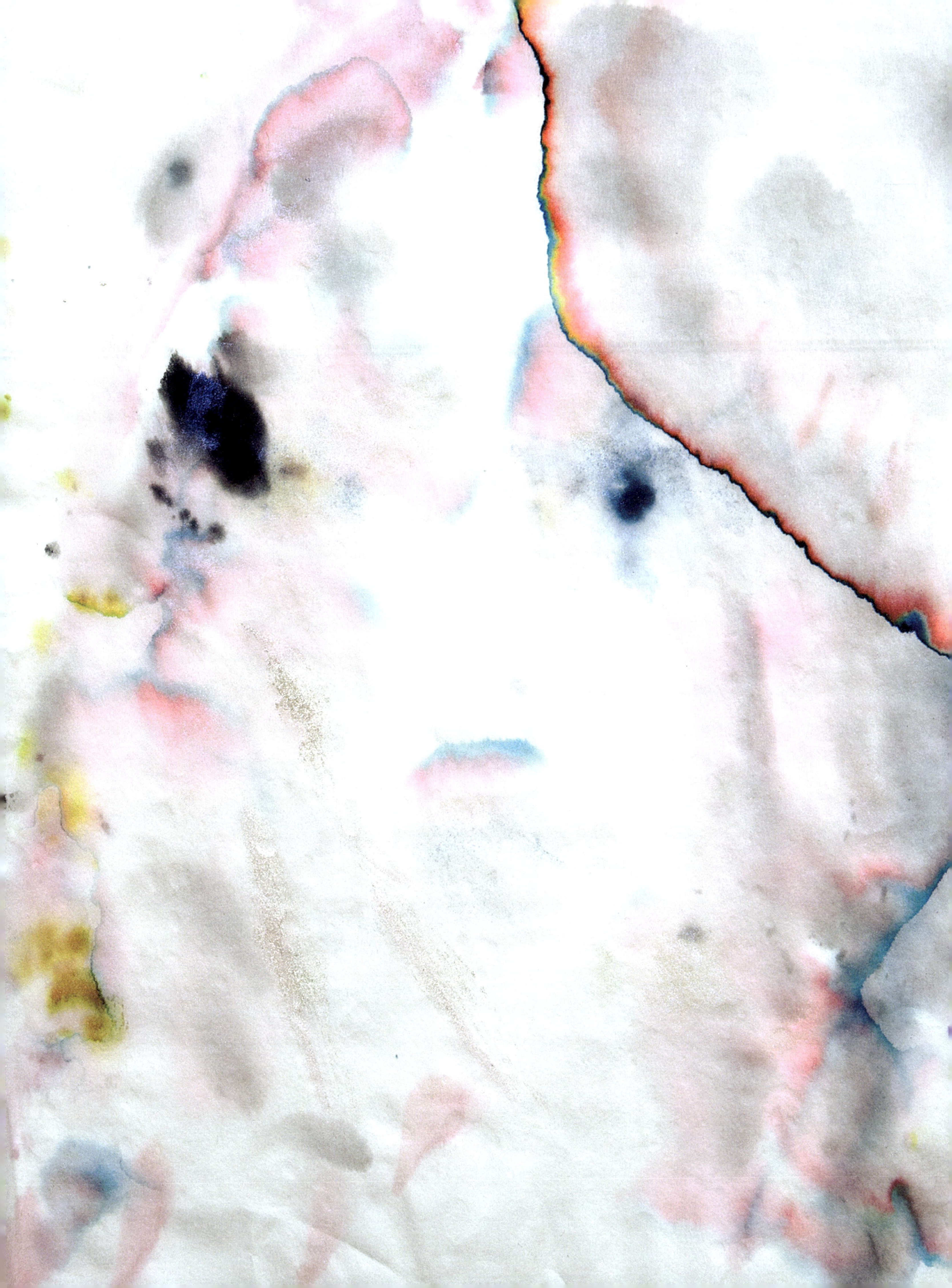

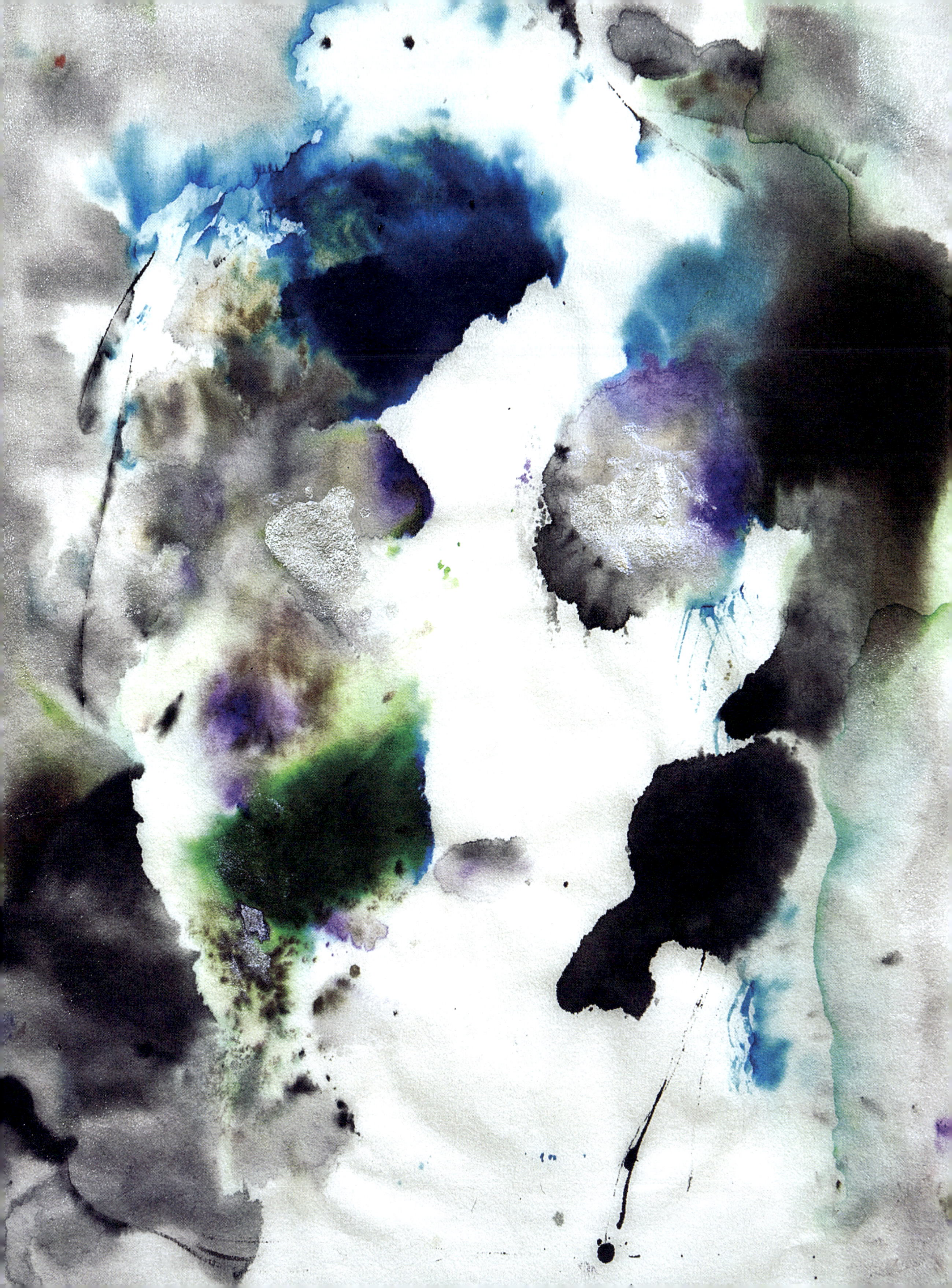

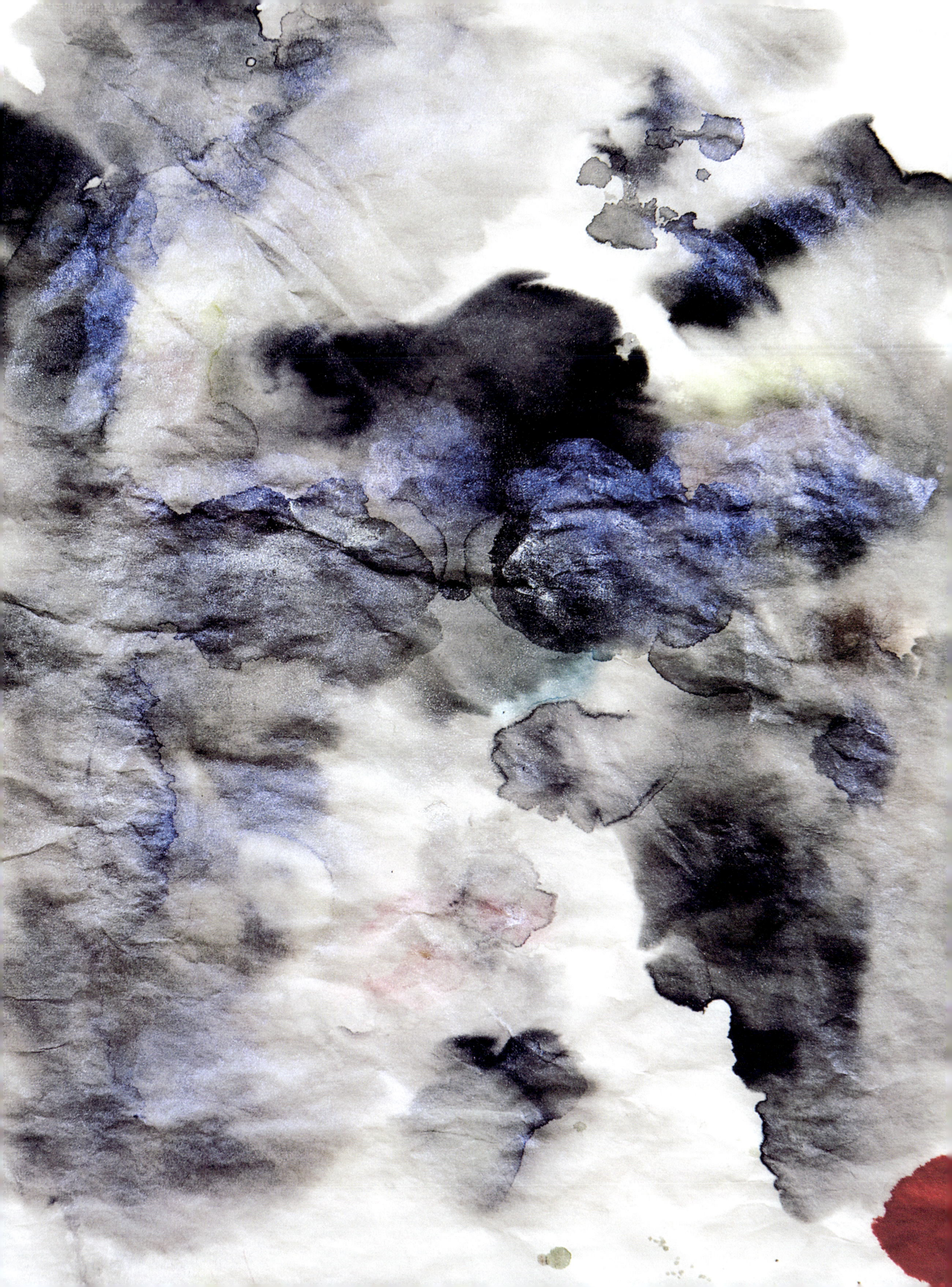

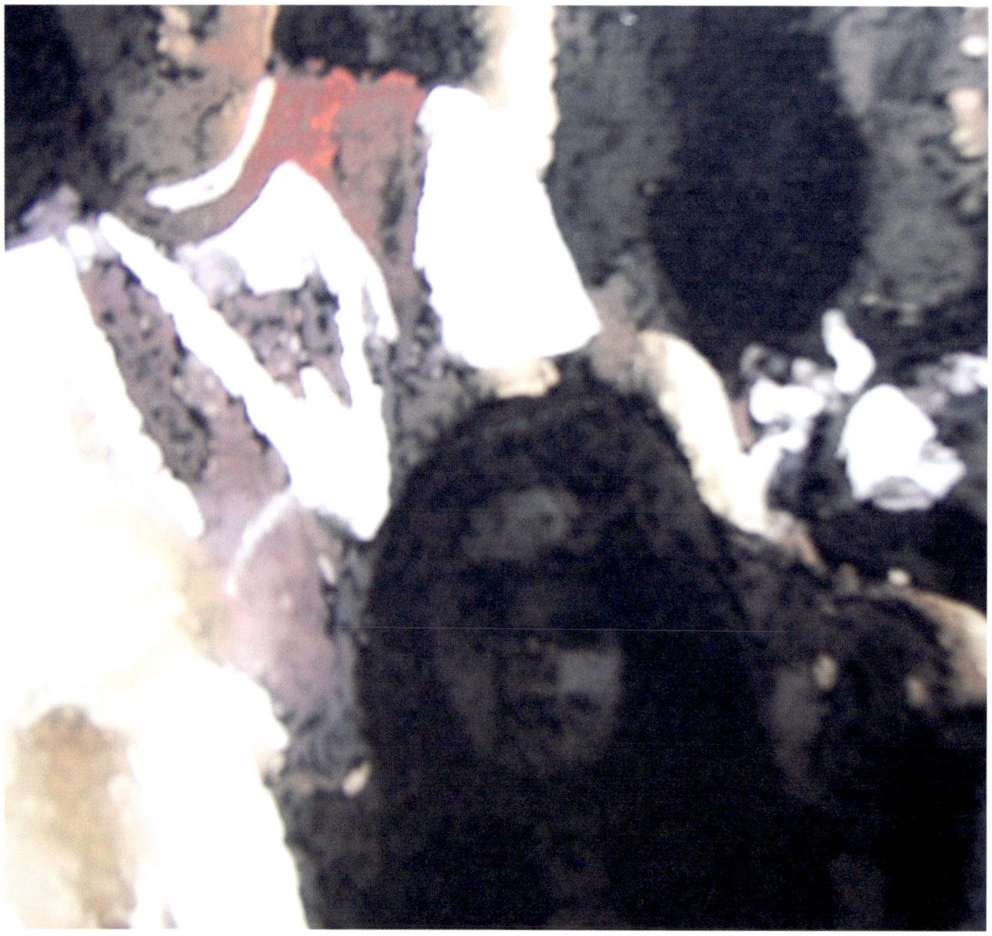

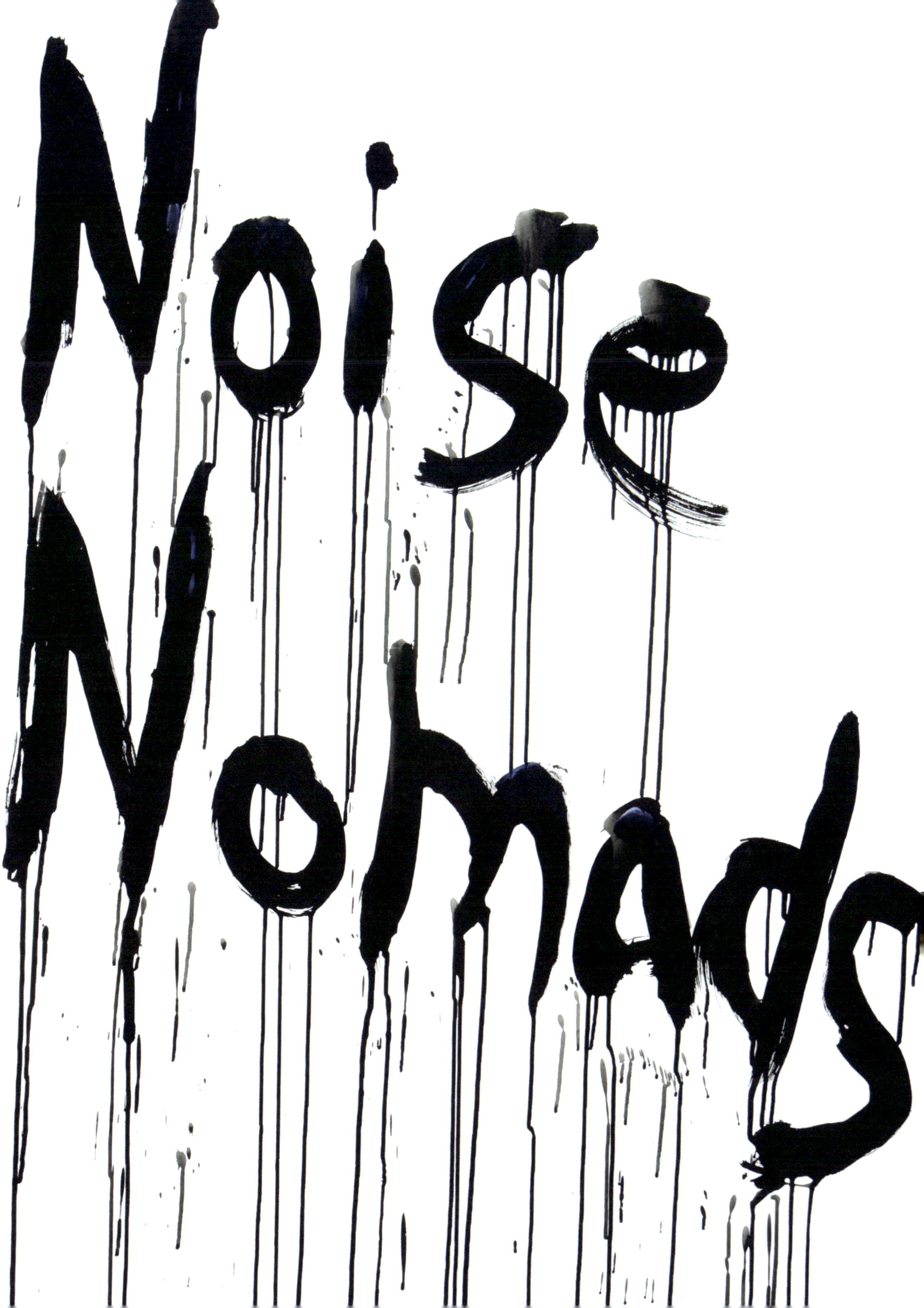
Noise
Nomads

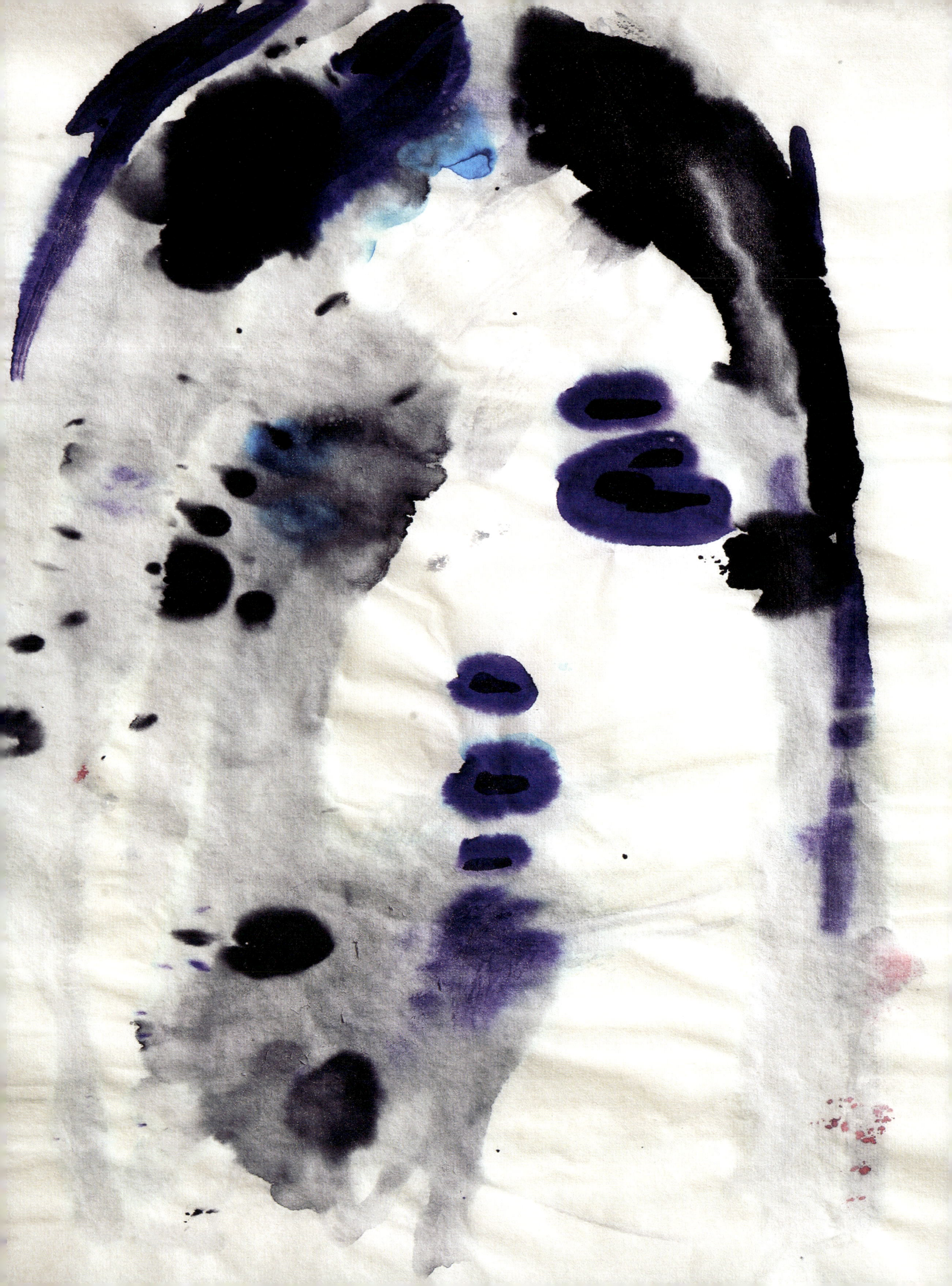

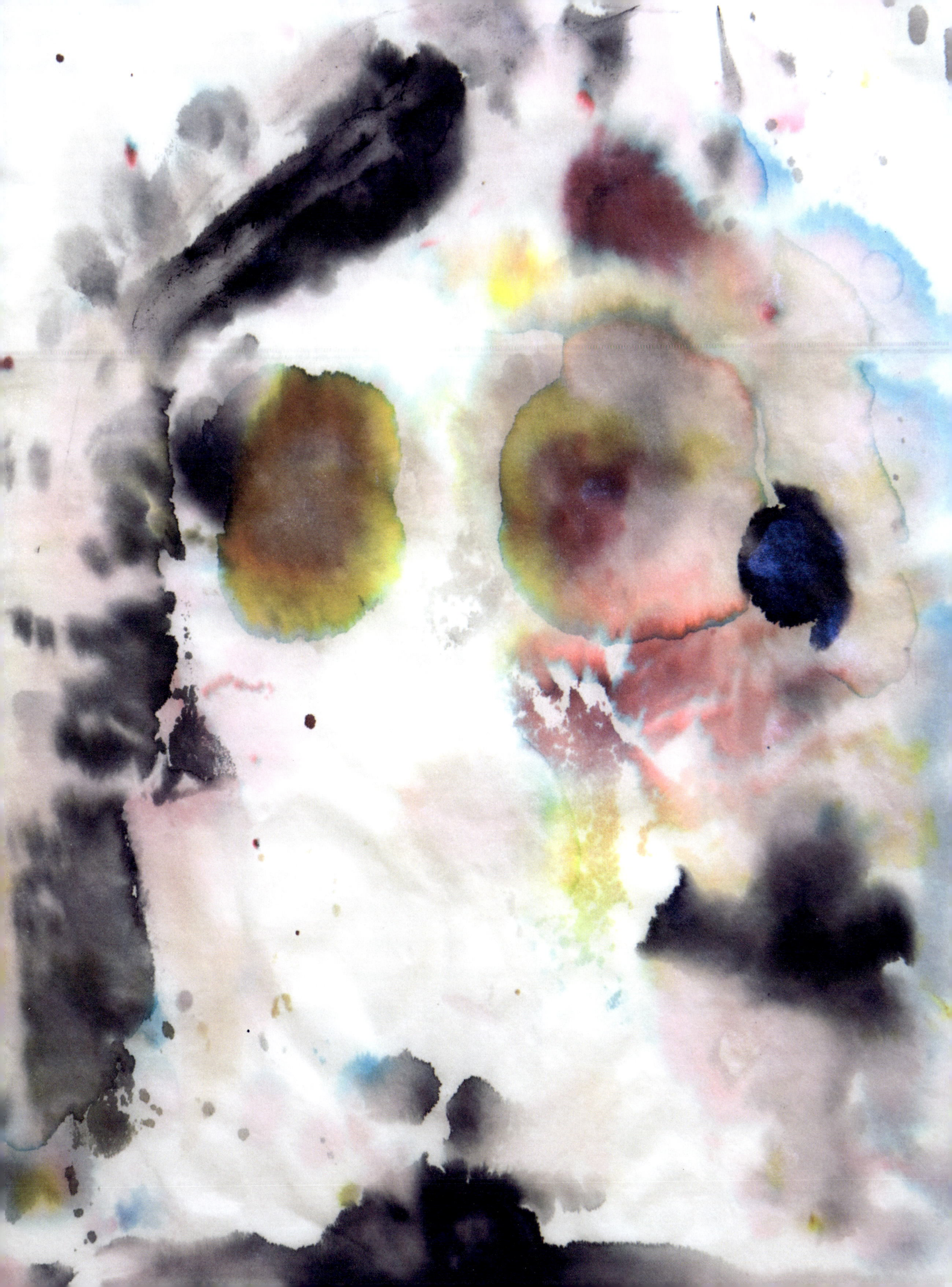

Looking out into the audience light comes from the projector at the back of the hall. It makes the back of peoples' heads look illuminated, like saints. The projector changes and some of the faces disappear into the dark. The ones further back I can't see at all. Toward the front of the hall half cheeks appear dappled with swirling colors from the light show. I'm trying not to look directly at anyone in the front so the spell of concentration won't be broken. Instead they appear as a collective mood. Suddenly something whirs by my head and smashes onto the stage. It's a cassette. I'm spinning around in a circle trying not to get dizzy but liking the dizziness of the blurry images. It looks like a flicker camera in 360 degrees. I wish I had a camera to record like it looks like.

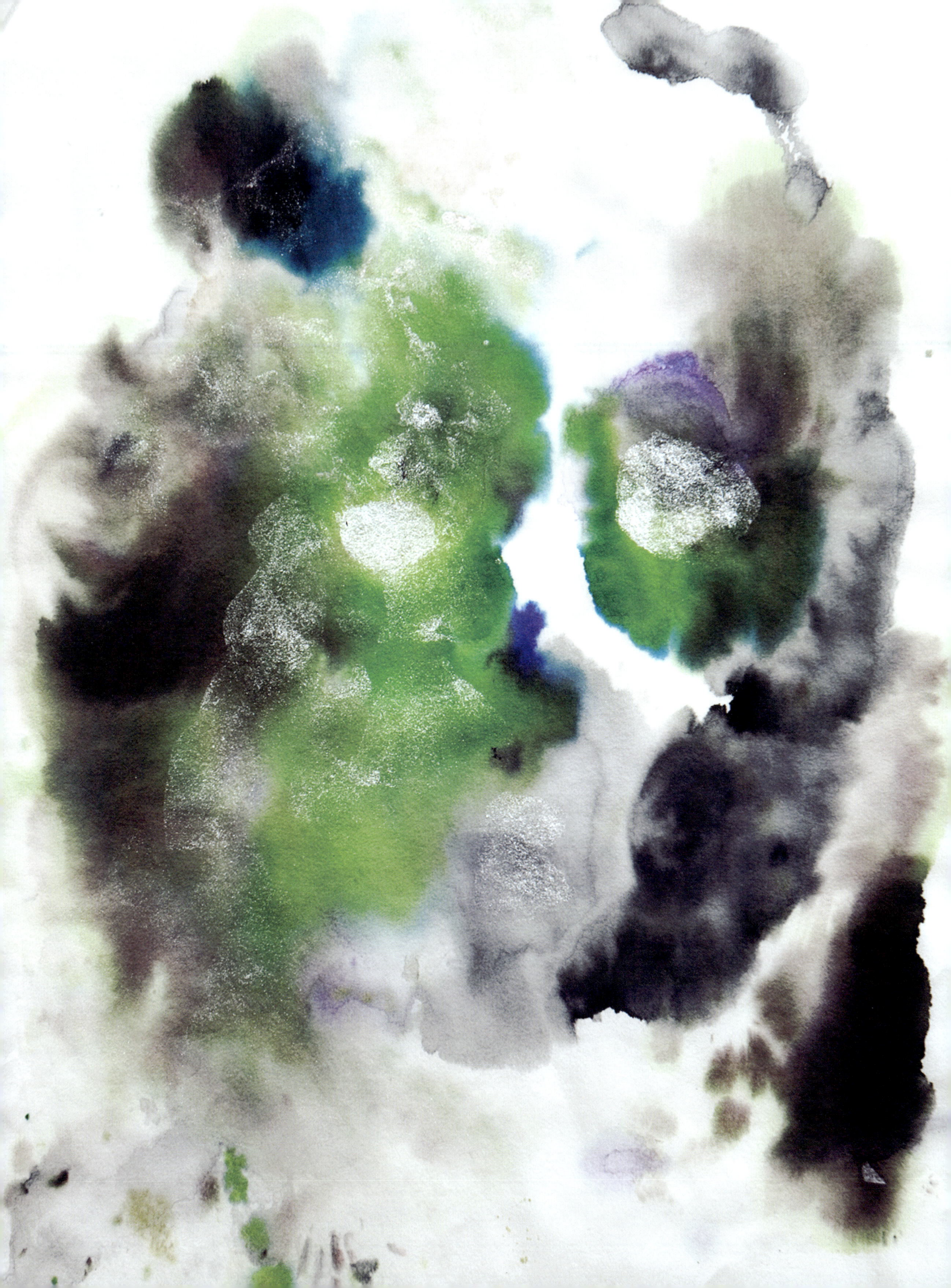

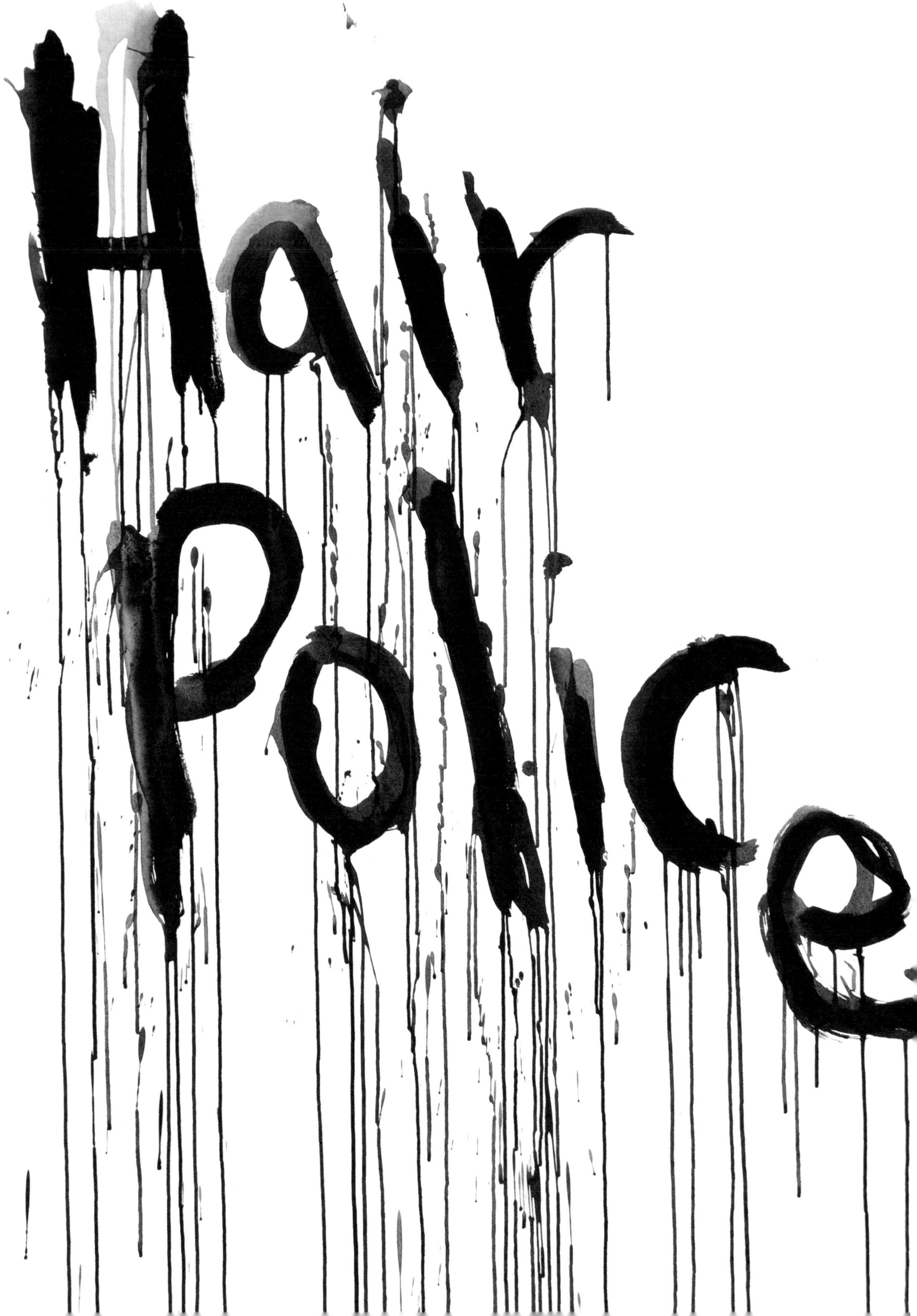
Hair
Police

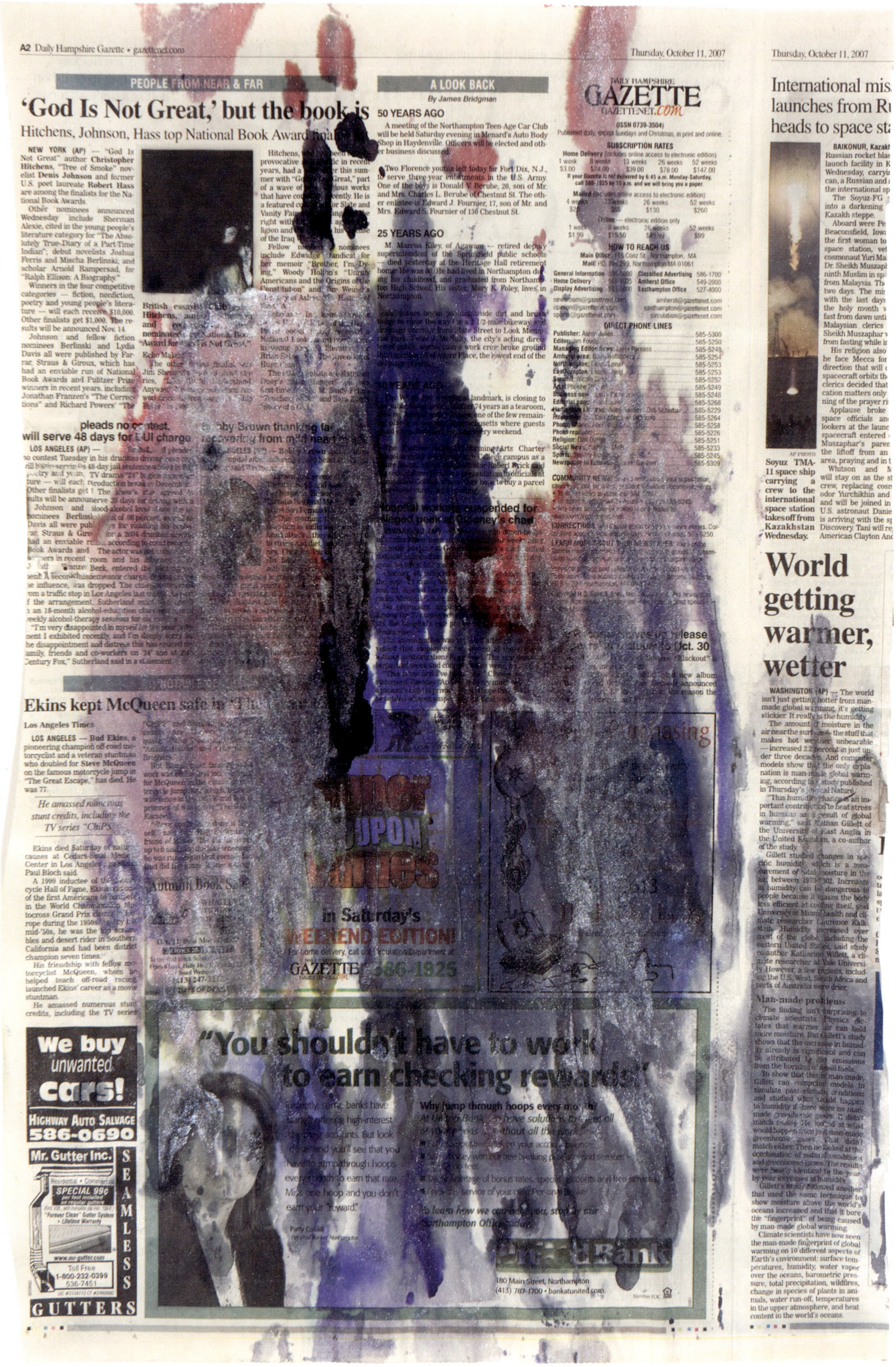

A2 Daily Hampshire Gazette • gazettenet.com

Thursday, October 11, 2007

Thursday, October 11, 2007

PEOPLE FROM NEAR & FAR

'God Is Not Great,' but the book is

Hitchens, Johnson, Hass top National Book Award finalists

NEW YORK (AP) — "God Is Not Great" author Christopher Hitchens, "Tree of Smoke" novelist Denis Johnson and former U.S. poet laureate Robert Hass are among the finalists for the National Book Awards.

Other nominees announced Wednesday include Sherman Alexie, cited in the young people's literature category for "The Absolutely True Diary of a Part-Time Indian"; debut novelists Joshua Ferris and Mischa Berlinski; and scholar Arnold Rampersad, for "Ralph Ellison: A Biography."

Winners in the four competitive categories — fiction, nonfiction, poetry and young people's literature — will each receive $10,000. Other finalists get $1,000. The results will be announced Nov. 14.

Johnson and fellow fiction nominees Berlinski and Lydia Davis all were published by Farrar, Straus & Giroux, which has had an enviable run of National Book Awards and Pulitzer Prize winners in recent years, including Jonathan Franzen's "The Corrections" and Richard Powers' "The

Hitchens, ... provocative ... in recent years, had a ... this summer with "God ... Great," part of a wave of ... works that have ... He is a featured ... Vanity Fair ... right with ... ligion and ... of the Iraq ...

Fellow ... nominees include Edwidge Danticat for her memoir "Brother, I'm Dying," Woody Holton's "Unruly Americans and the Origins of the Constitution" and Tim Weiner's ...

British essayist ... Hitchens ... and ... nominated ... National Book Award for "God Is Not Great."

Echo Maker ...

A LOOK BACK

By James Bridgman

50 YEARS AGO

A meeting of the Northampton Teen Age Car Club will be held Saturday evening in Menard's Auto Body Shop in Haydenville. Officers will be elected and other business discussed.

Two Florence youths left today for Fort Dix, N.J., to serve three-year enlistments in the U.S. Army. One of the boys is Donald V. Berube, 20, son of Mr. and Mrs. Charles L. Berube of Chestnut St. The other enlistee is Edward J. Fournier, 17, son of Mr. and Mrs. Edward S. Fournier of 136 Chestnut St.

25 YEARS AGO

M. Marcus Kiley, of Agawam — retired deputy superintendent of the Springfield public schools — died yesterday at the Heritage Hall retirement home. He was 8... He had lived in Northampton du... ing his childhood, and graduated from Northampton High School. His sister, Mary K. Foley, lives in Northampton.

... landmark, is closing to ... 74 years as a tearoom, ... one of the few remain... ...usetts where guests ... ery weekend.

Hospital workers suspended for alleged peek at Clooney's chart

DAILY HAMPSHIRE GAZETTE GAZETTENET.com

(ISSN 0739-3504)

Published daily, except Sundays and Christmas, in print and online.

SUBSCRIPTION RATES

Home Delivery (includes online access to electronic edition)

1 week	8 weeks	13 weeks	26 weeks	52 weeks
$3.00	$24.00	$39.00	$78.00	$147.00

If your Gazette is not delivered by 6:45 a.m. Monday-Saturday, call 586-1925 by 10 a.m. and we will bring you a paper.

Mailed (includes online access to electronic edition)

HOW TO REACH US

Main Office: 115 Conz St., Northampton, MA

Mail: P.O. Box 299, Northampton MA 01061

DIRECT PHONE LINES

... pleads no contest, will serve 48 days for DUI charge

LOS ANGELES (AP) — ...

Bobby Brown thanking fans ... recovering from mild heart ...

Ekins kept McQueen safe in 'The Great Escape'

Los Angeles Times

LOS ANGELES — Bud Ekins, a pioneering champion off-road motorcyclist and a veteran stuntman who doubled for Steve McQueen on the famous motorcycle jump in "The Great Escape," has died. He was 77.

He amassed numerous stunt credits, including the TV series "ChiPS"

Ekins died Saturday of natural causes at Cedars-Sinai Medical Center in Los Angeles, ... Paul Bloch said.

A 1999 inductee of the ... cycle Hall of Fame, Ekins ... of the first Americans to ... in the World Championship ... tocross Grand Prix ... rope during the 1950s ... mid-'50s, he was the top ... bles and desert rider in Southern California and had been district champion seven times.

His friendship with fellow motorcyclist McQueen, whom he helped teach off-road racing, launched Ekins' career as a movie stuntman.

He amassed numerous stunt credits, including the TV series

Autumn Book Sale

in Saturday's WEEKEND EDITION!

GAZETTE 586-1925

We buy unwanted cars! HIGHWAY AUTO SALVAGE 586-0690

Mr. Gutter Inc. SEAMLESS GUTTERS

Toll Free 1-800-232-0399 536-7451

"You shouldn't have to work to earn checking rewards!"

Why jump through hoops every month?

180 Main Street, Northampton (413) 787-1700 • bankatunited.com

International mis... launches from Ru... heads to space sta...

BAIKONUR, Kazakh... Russian rocket bla... launch facility in K... Wednesday, carryin... can, a Russian and a... the international sp...

Soyuz TMA-11 space ship carrying a crew to the international space station takes off from Kazakhstan Wednesday.

World getting warmer, wetter

WASHINGTON (AP) — The world isn't just getting hotter from man-made global warming, it's getting stickier. It really is the humidity.

The amount of moisture in the air near the surface — the stuff that makes hot weather unbearable — increased 2.2 percent in just under three decades. And computer models show that the only explanation is man-made global warming, according to a study published in Thursday's journal Nature.

Man-made problems

Climate scientists have now seen the man-made fingerprint of global warming on 10 different aspects of Earth's environment: surface temperatures, humidity, water vapor over the oceans, barometric pressure, total precipitation, wildfires, change in species of plants in animals, water run-off, temperatures in the upper atmosphere, and heat content in the world's oceans.

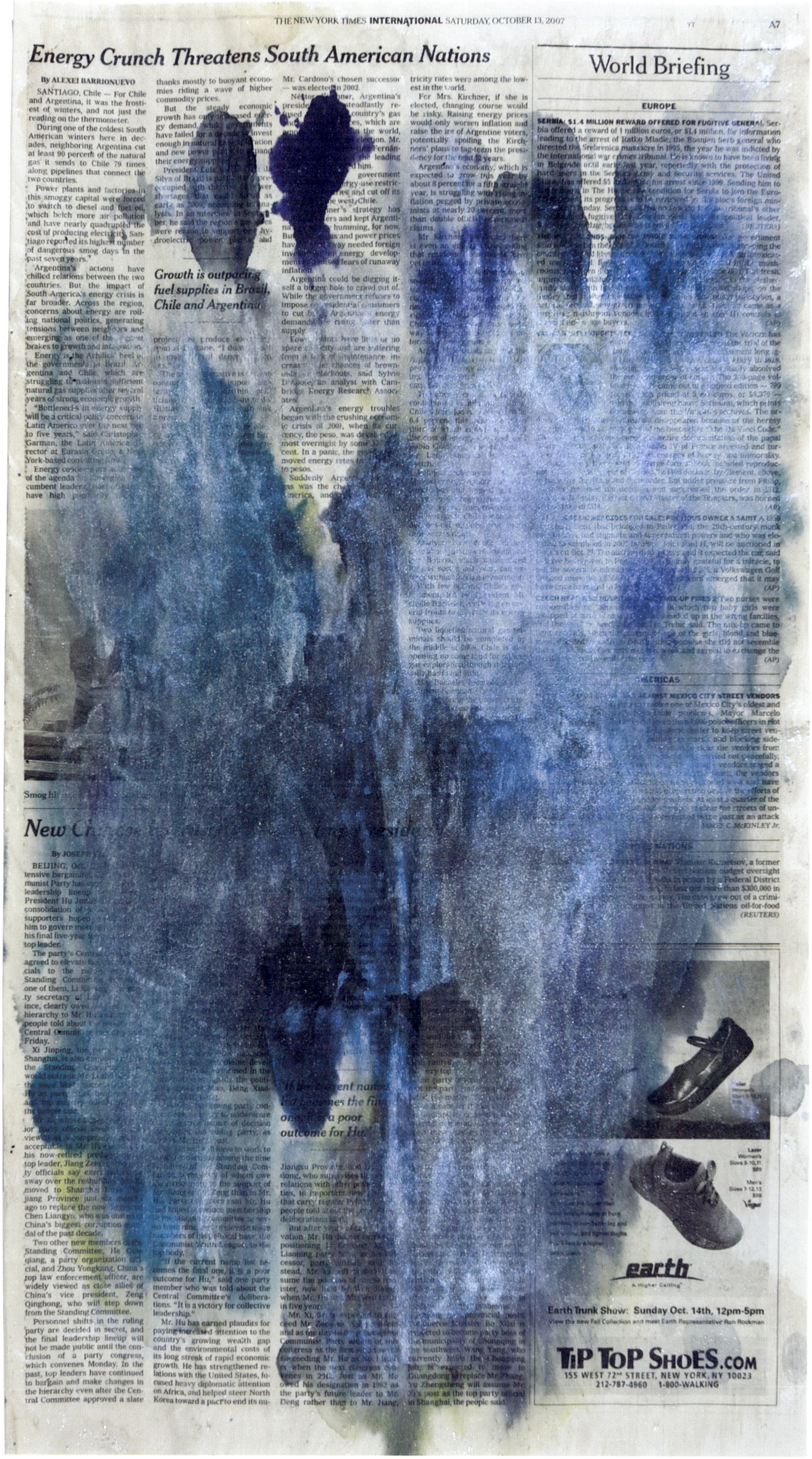
THE NEW YORK TIMES INTERNATIONAL SATURDAY, OCTOBER 13, 2007
A7
Energy Crunch Threatens South American Nations
By ALEXEI BARRIONUEVO
Growth is outpacing fuel supplies in Brazil, Chile and Argentina.
World Briefing
EUROPE
SERBIA: $1.4 MILLION REWARD OFFERED FOR FUGITIVE GENERAL
earth
Earth Trunk Show: Sunday Oct. 14th, 12pm-5pm
TIP TOP SHOES.COM
155 WEST 72ND STREET, NEW YORK, NY 10023
212-787-4960 1-800-WALKING

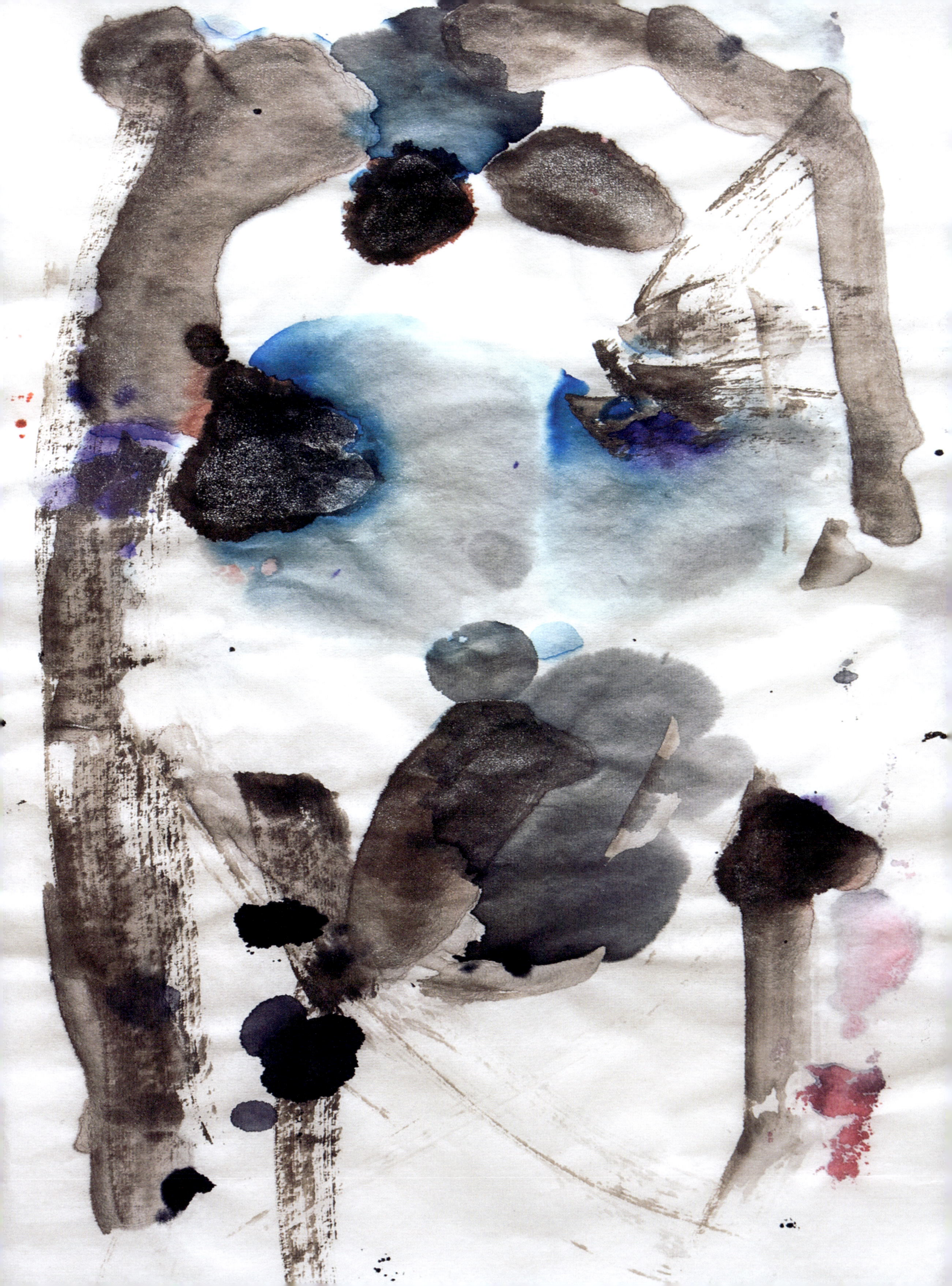

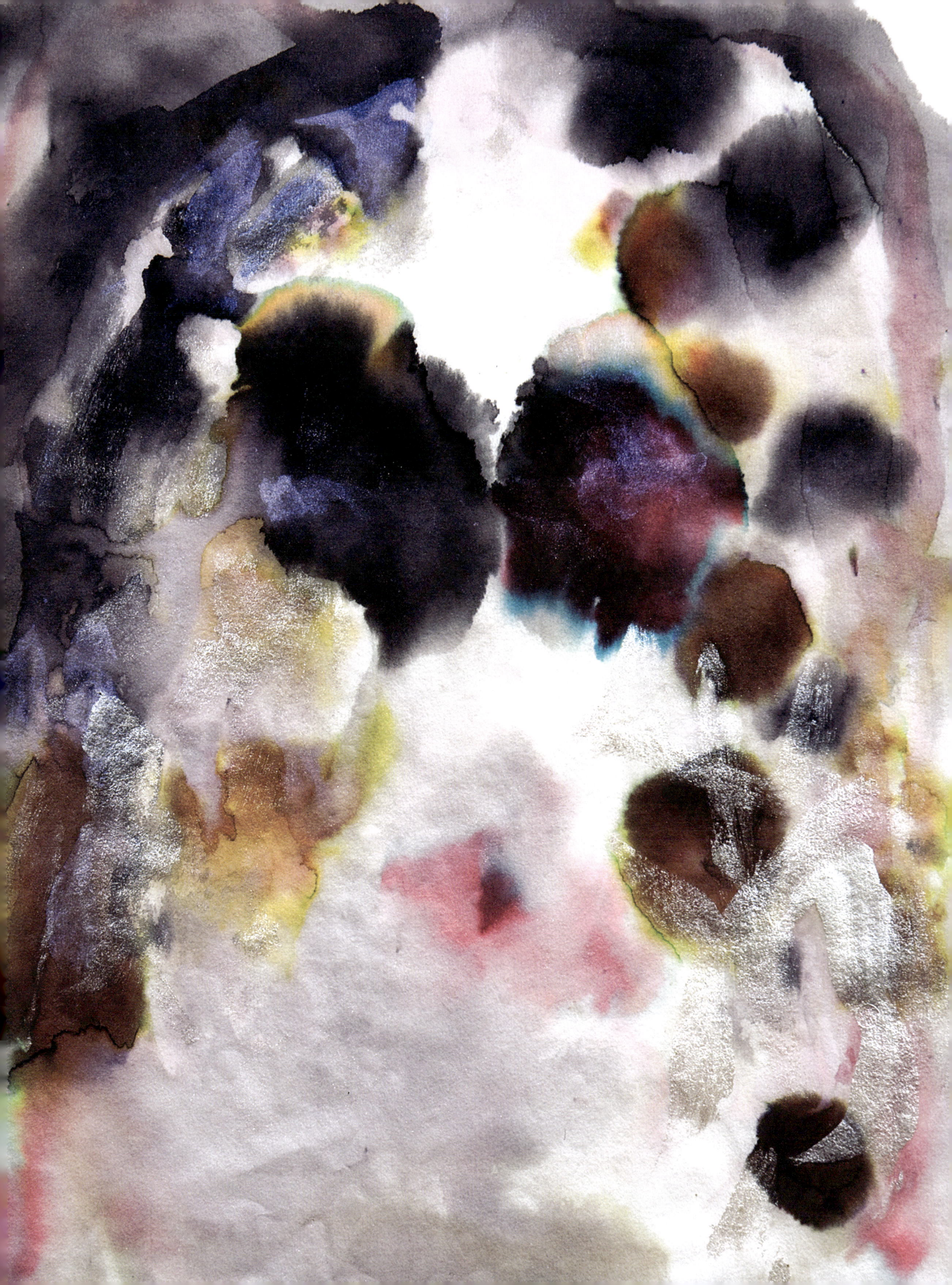

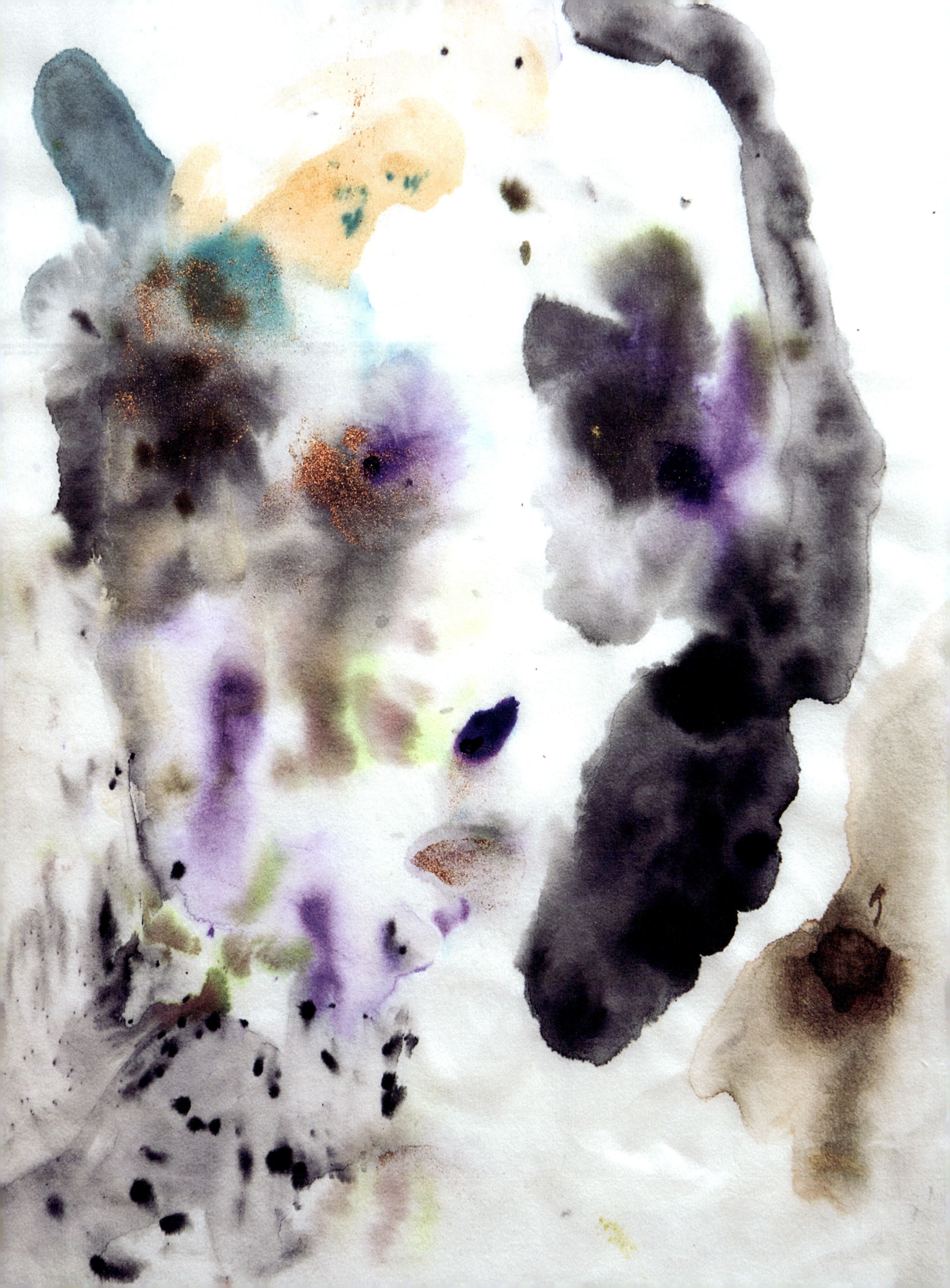

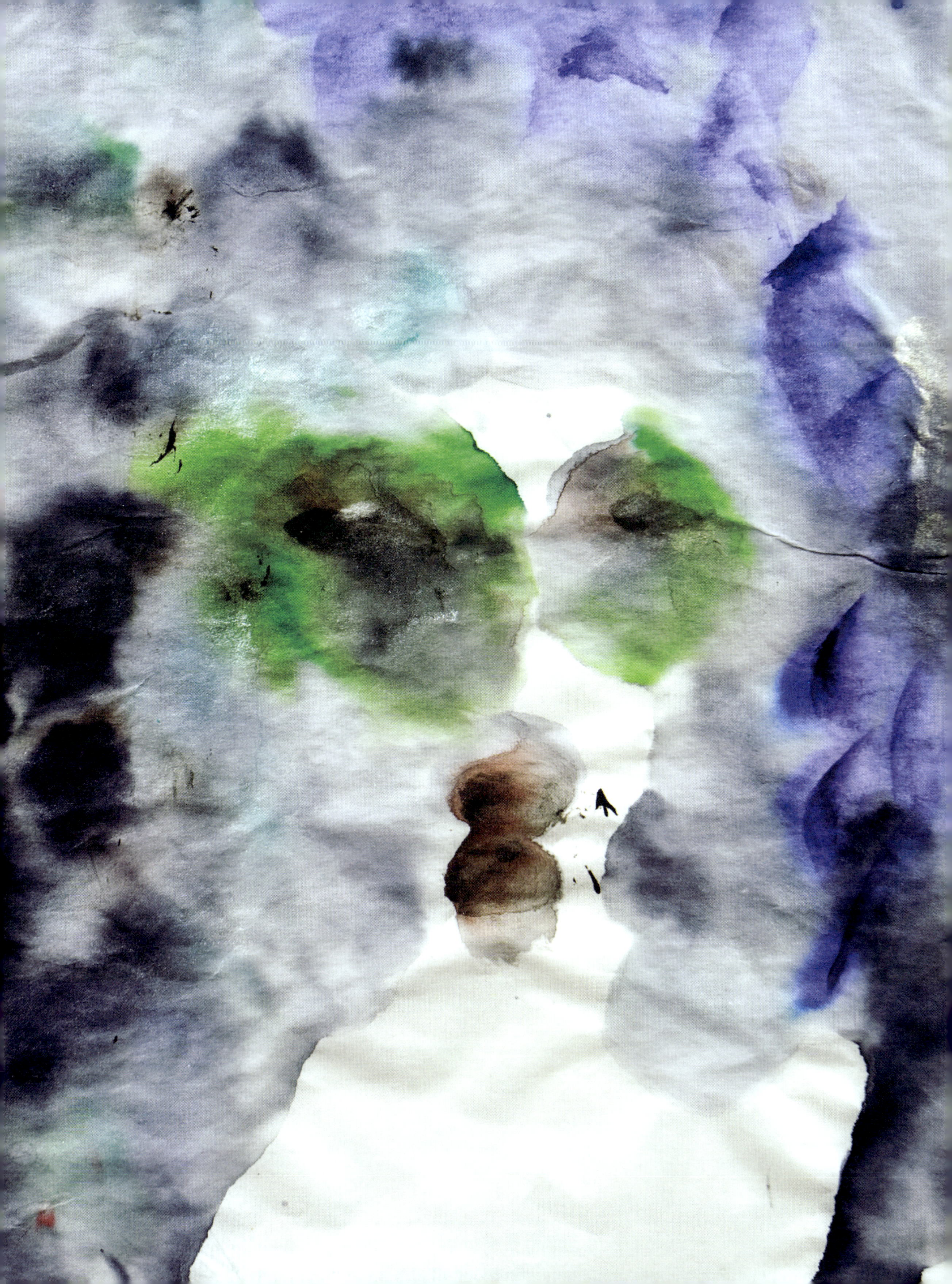

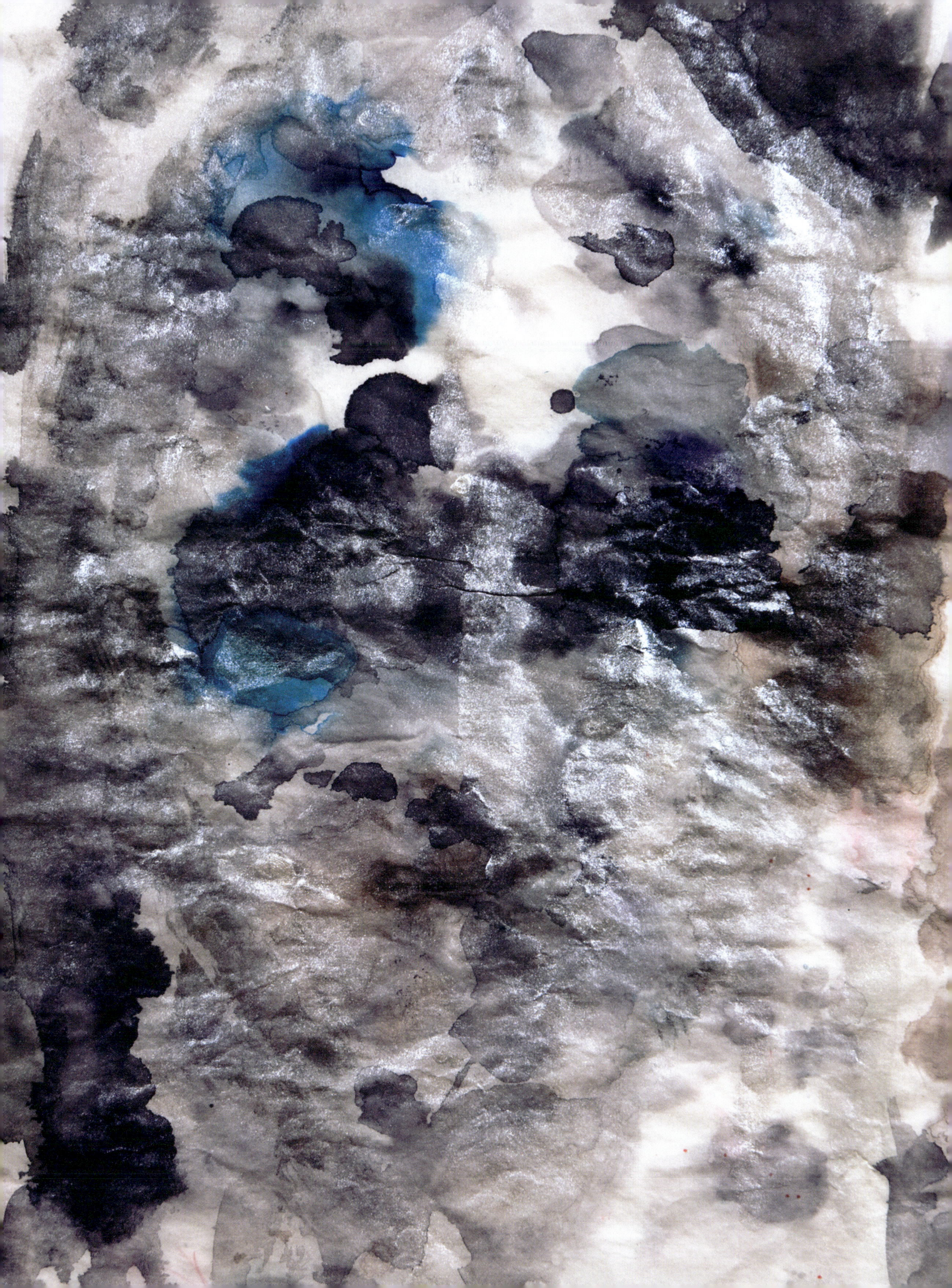

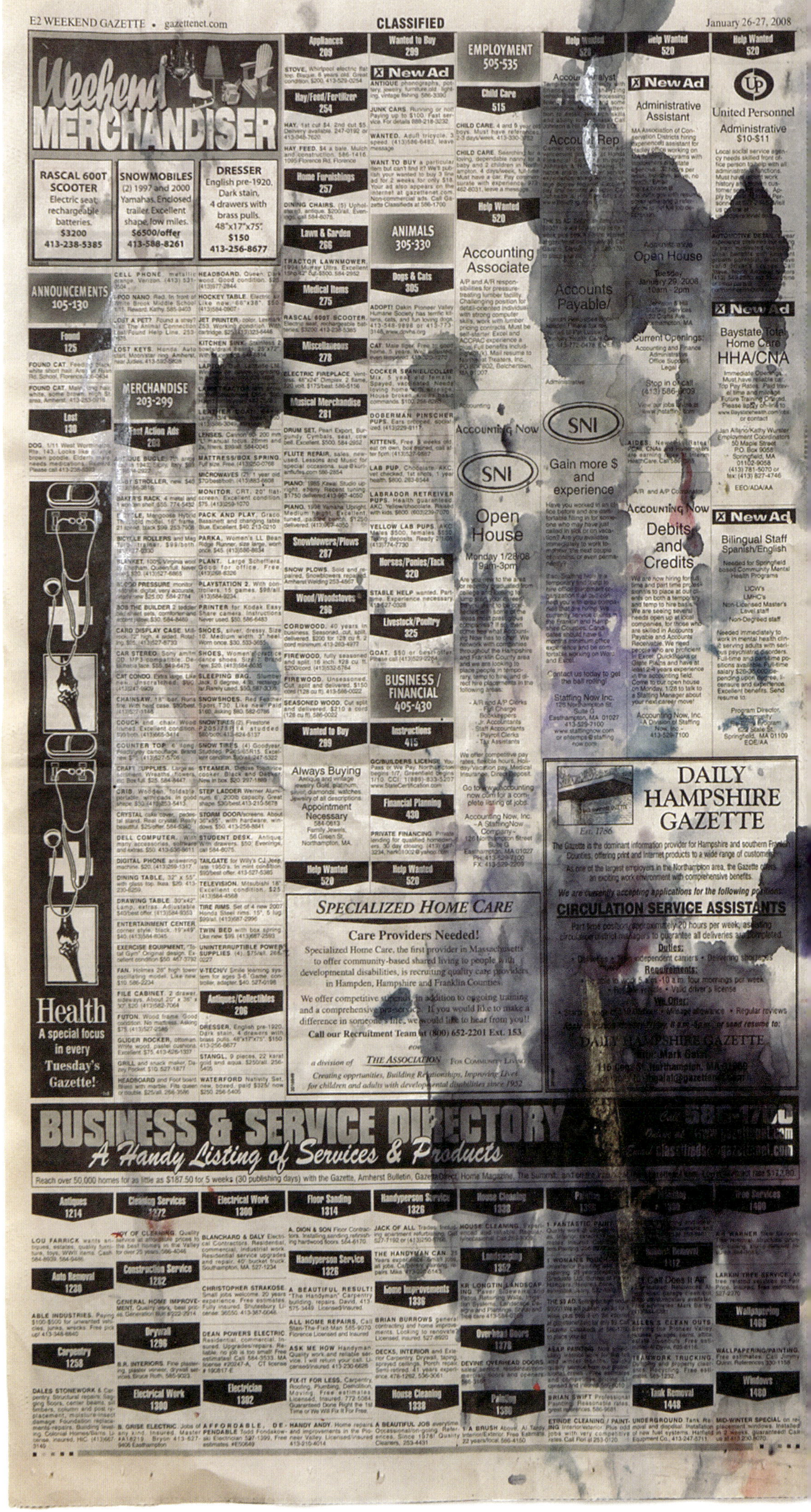
E2 WEEKEND GAZETTE • gazettenet.com

CLASSIFIED

January 26-27, 2008

Weekend MERCHANDISER

RASCAL 600T SCOOTER
Electric seat, rechargeable batteries.
$3200
413-238-5385

SNOWMOBILES
(2) 1997 and 2000 Yamahas. Enclosed trailer. Excellent shape, low miles.
$6500/offer
413-588-8261

DRESSER
English pre-1920. Dark stain, 4 drawers with brass pulls. 48"x17"x75".
$150
413-256-8677

ANNOUNCEMENTS 105-130

Found 125

Lost 130

MERCHANDISE 203-299

Health
A special focus in every Tuesday's Gazette!

Appliances 209

Hay/Feed/Fertilizer 254

Home Furnishings 257

Lawn & Garden 266

Medical Items 275

Miscellaneous 278

Musical Merchandise 281

Snowblowers/Plows 287

Wood/Woodstoves 296

Wanted to Buy 299

Antiques/Collectibles 206

Help Wanted 520

Wanted to Buy 299

New Ad

ANIMALS 305-330

Dogs & Cats 305

Horses/Ponies/Tack 320

Livestock/Poultry 325

BUSINESS / FINANCIAL 405-430

Instructions 415

Financial Planning 430

Help Wanted 520

Always Buying
Antique and vintage jewelry. Gold, platinum, silver, diamonds, watches. Jewelry of all descriptions.
Appointment Necessary
584-0613
Family Jewels
56 Green St., Northampton, MA

EMPLOYMENT 505-535

Child Care 515

Help Wanted 520

Accounting Associate

Open House
Monday 1/28/08
9am-3pm

SNI

Accounting Now

Help Wanted 520

Accounts Payable

Account Rep

Gain more $ and experience

Help Wanted 520

New Ad

Administrative Assistant

Open House

Accounting Now

Debits and Credits

Help Wanted 520

United Personnel

Administrative
$10-$11

New Ad

Baystate Total Home Care
HHA/CNA

New Ad

Bilingual Staff
Spanish/English

SPECIALIZED HOME CARE

Care Providers Needed!

Specialized Home Care, the first provider in Massachusetts to offer community-based shared living to people with developmental disabilities, is recruiting quality care providers in Hampden, Hampshire and Franklin Counties.

We offer competitive stipends, in addition to ongoing training and a comprehensive process. If you would like to make a difference in someone's life, we would like to hear from you!

Call our Recruitment Team at (800) 652-2201 Ext. 153

a division of THE ASSOCIATION For Community Living

Creating opportunities, Building Relationships, Improving Lives for children and adults with developmental disabilities since 1952

DAILY HAMPSHIRE GAZETTE

Est. 1786

We are currently accepting applications for the following positions:

CIRCULATION SERVICE ASSISTANTS

BUSINESS & SERVICE DIRECTORY
A Handy Listing of Services & Products

Antiques 1214

Cleaning Services 1272

Electrical Work 1300

Floor Sanding 1314

Handyperson Service 1326

House Cleaning 1338

Auto Removal 1230

Construction Service 1282

Handyperson Service 1326

Landscaping 1352

Home Improvements 1336

Carpentry 1258

Drywall 1296

Overhead Doors 1378

Electrical Work 1300

Electrician 1302

House Cleaning 1338

Painting 1390

Tank Removal 1448

Wallpapering 1468

Windows 1480

Tree Services 1460

FAST ACTION ADS

Place your ad for merchandise *priced $99 or less* in the Classified Marketplace ... and sell it fast and

FREE!

- 1 item per [illegible]
- 1 ad per household per week
- **FREE ad published 6 consecutive days in the Gazette;**
  1 time in Amherst Bulletin;
  1 time in GazetteDirect;
  1 week on GazetteNet
- Non-commercial items only
- Pets excluded
- Ad must include item priced $99 or less and phone number
- If emailing your text, please include your name, address and daytime phone number
- Call us for complete details

DAILY HAMPSHIRE GAZETTE
GAZETTENET.com

AMHERST BULLETIN

Gazette Direct

*For **FAST** results, call*

586-1700

or email your text to classifieds@gazettenet.com
*or fax to **413-585-5293**. Be sure to include your name and daytime phone number.*

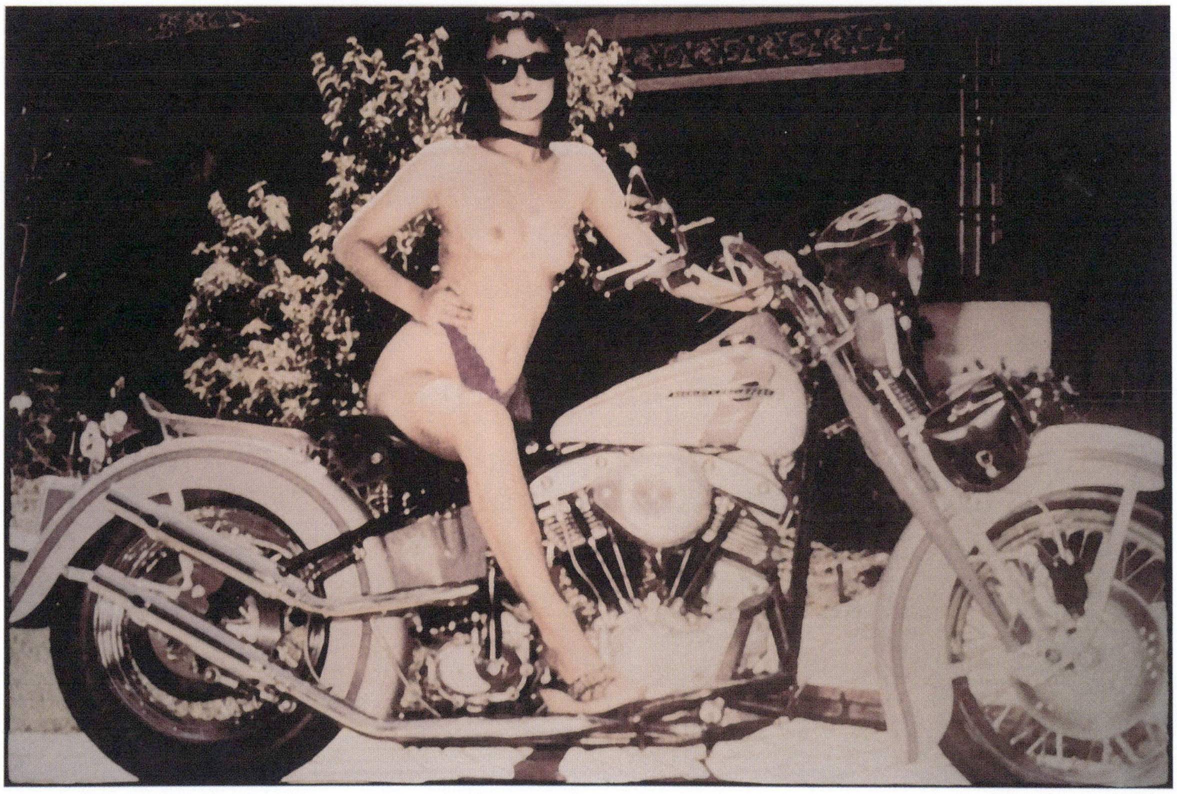

2007

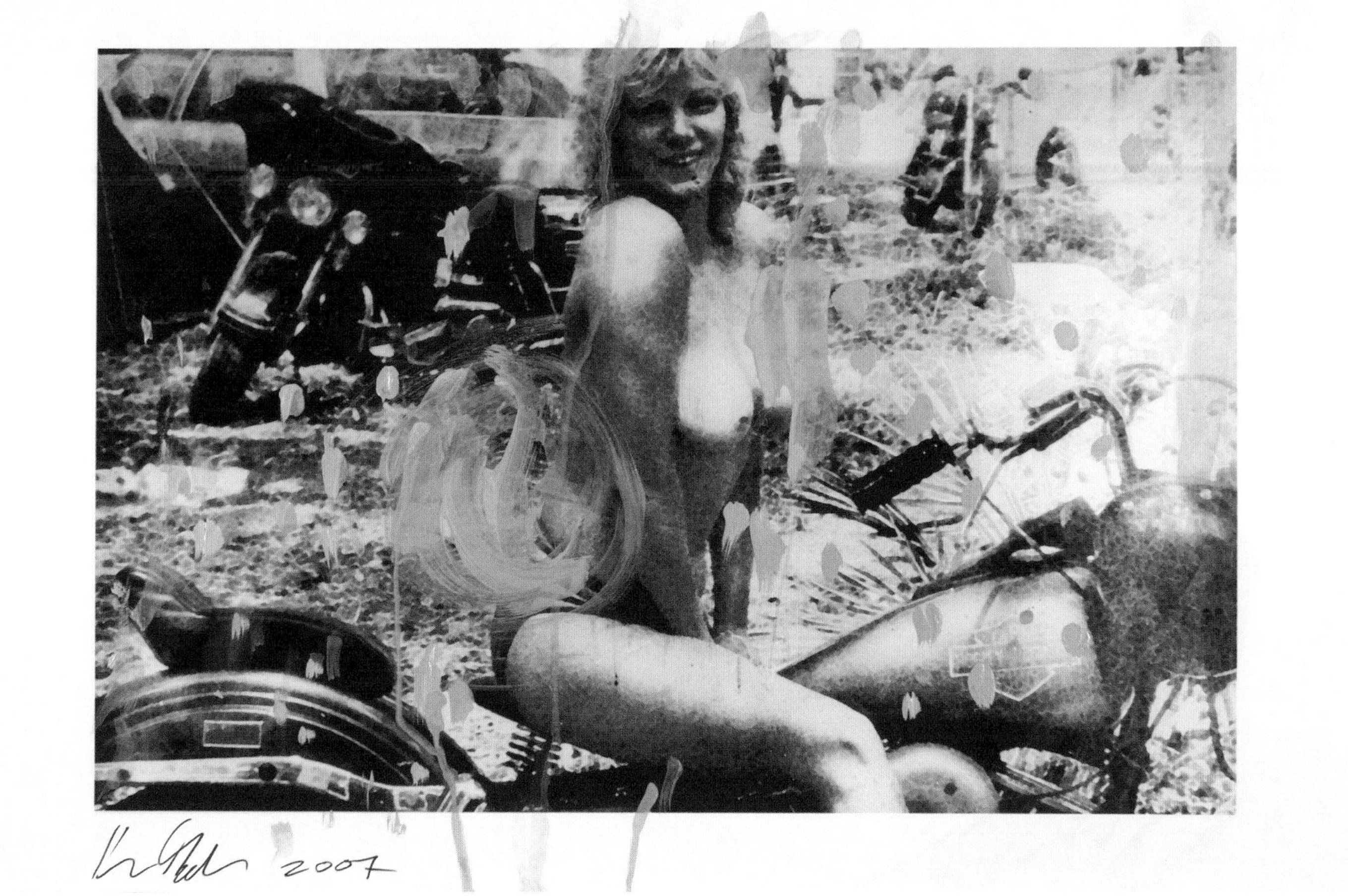
2007

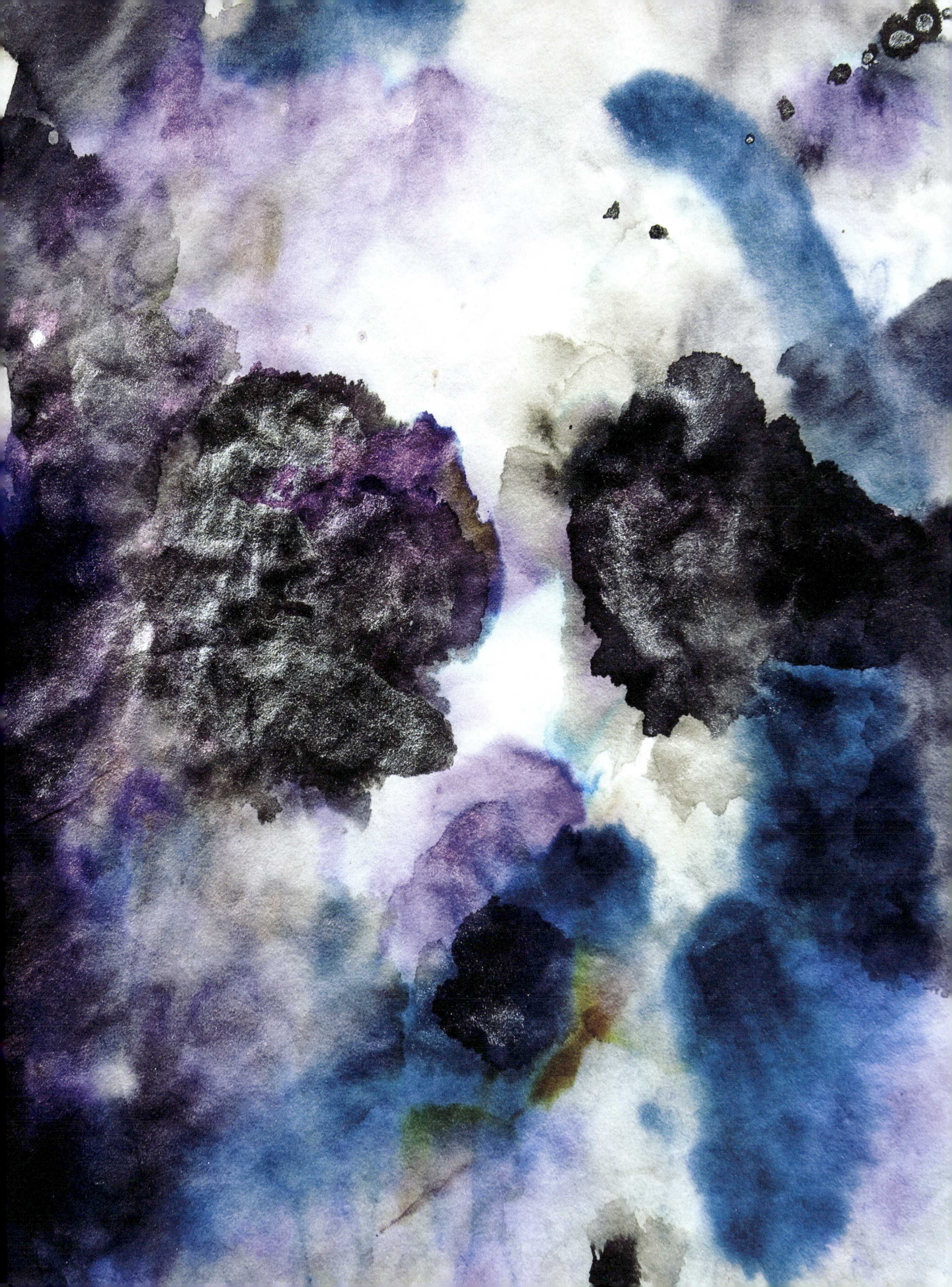

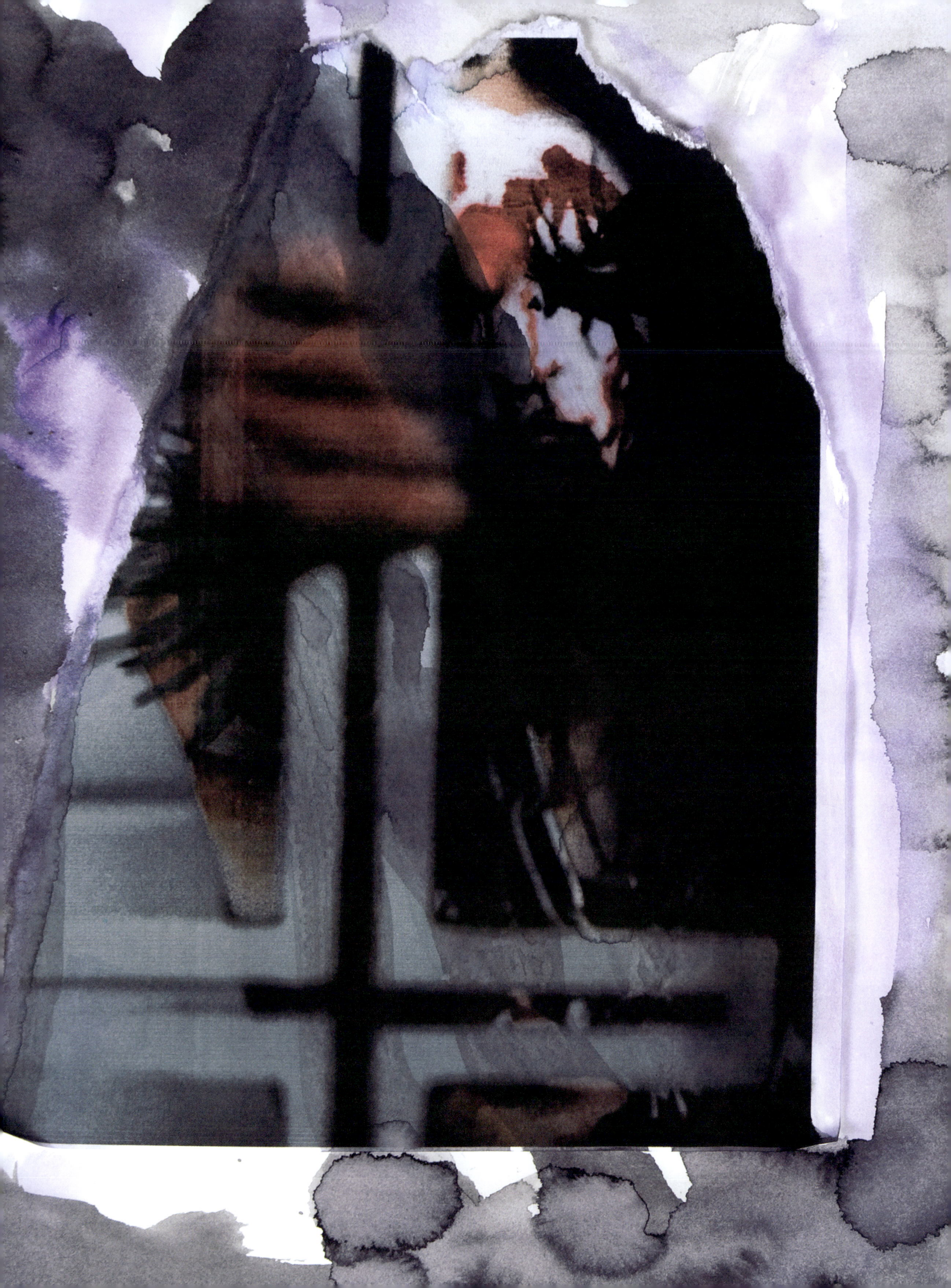

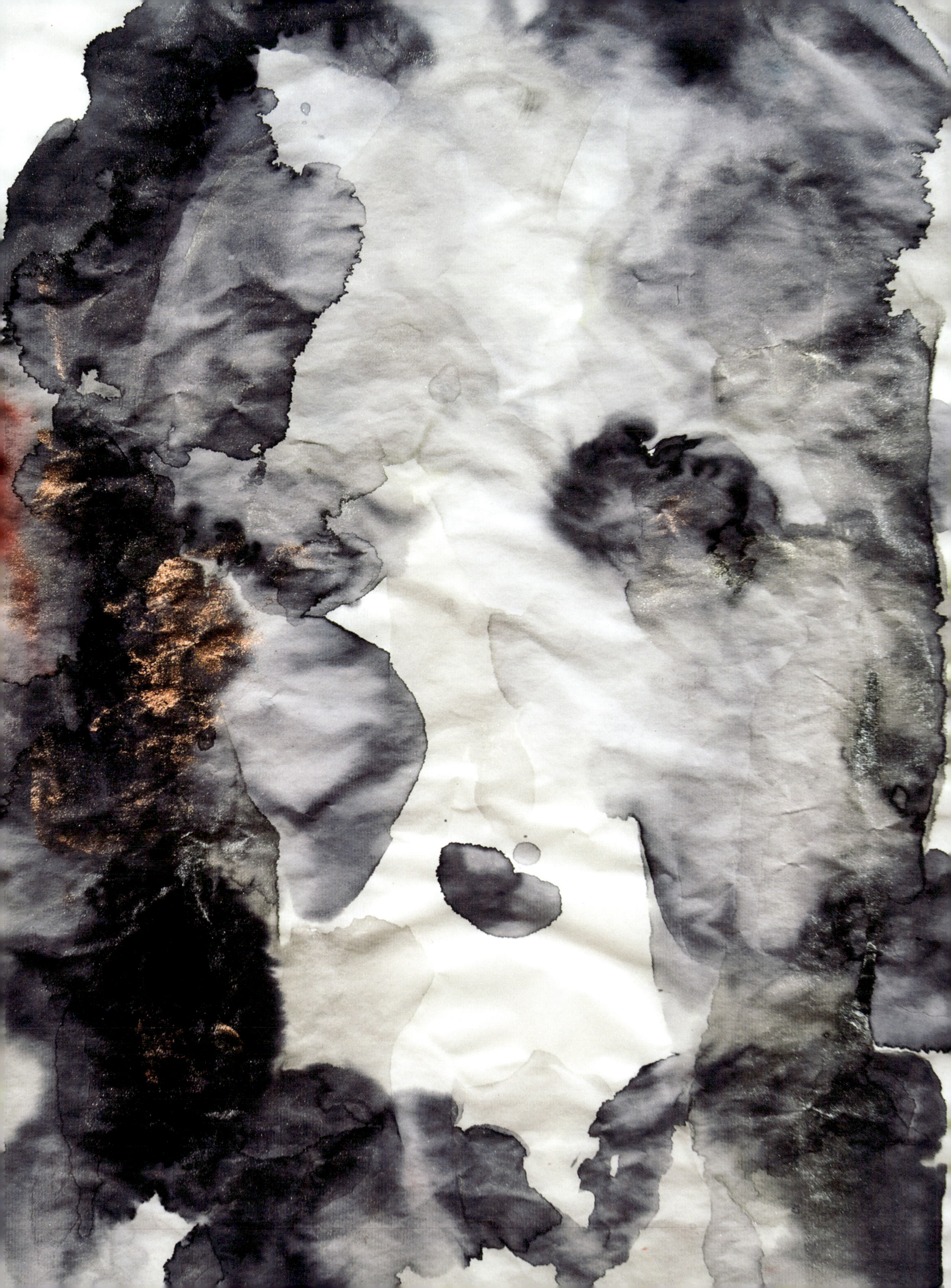

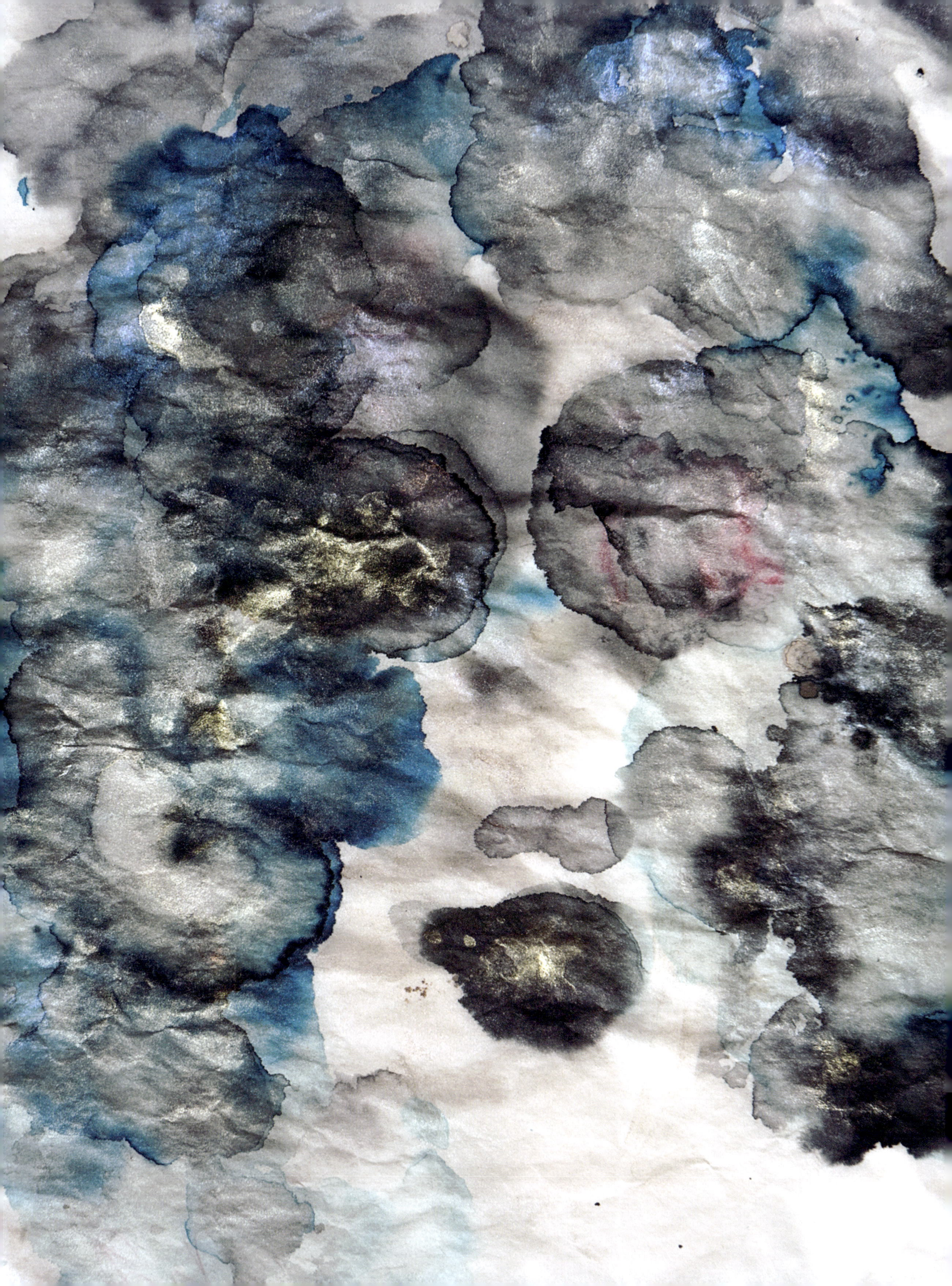

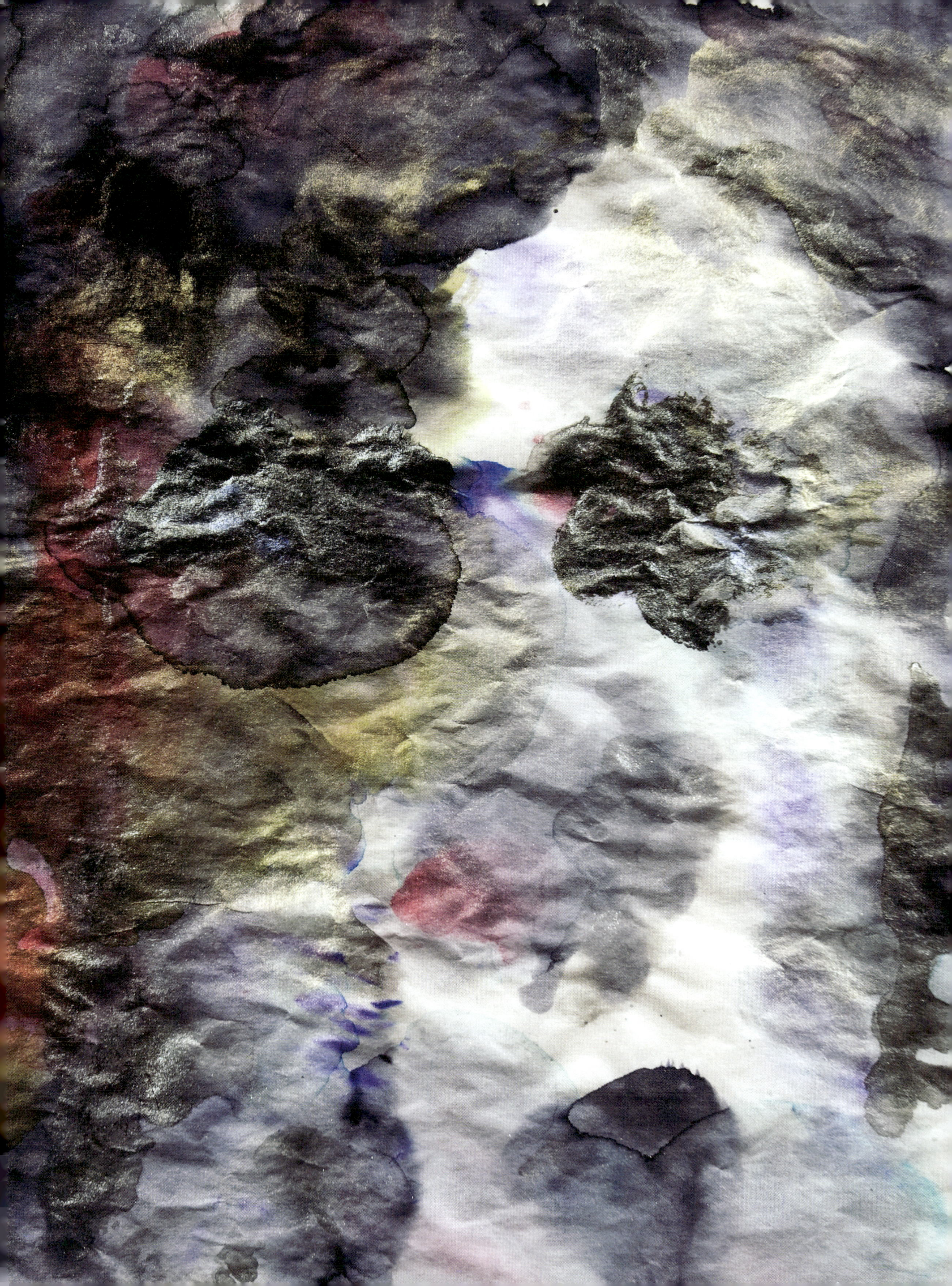

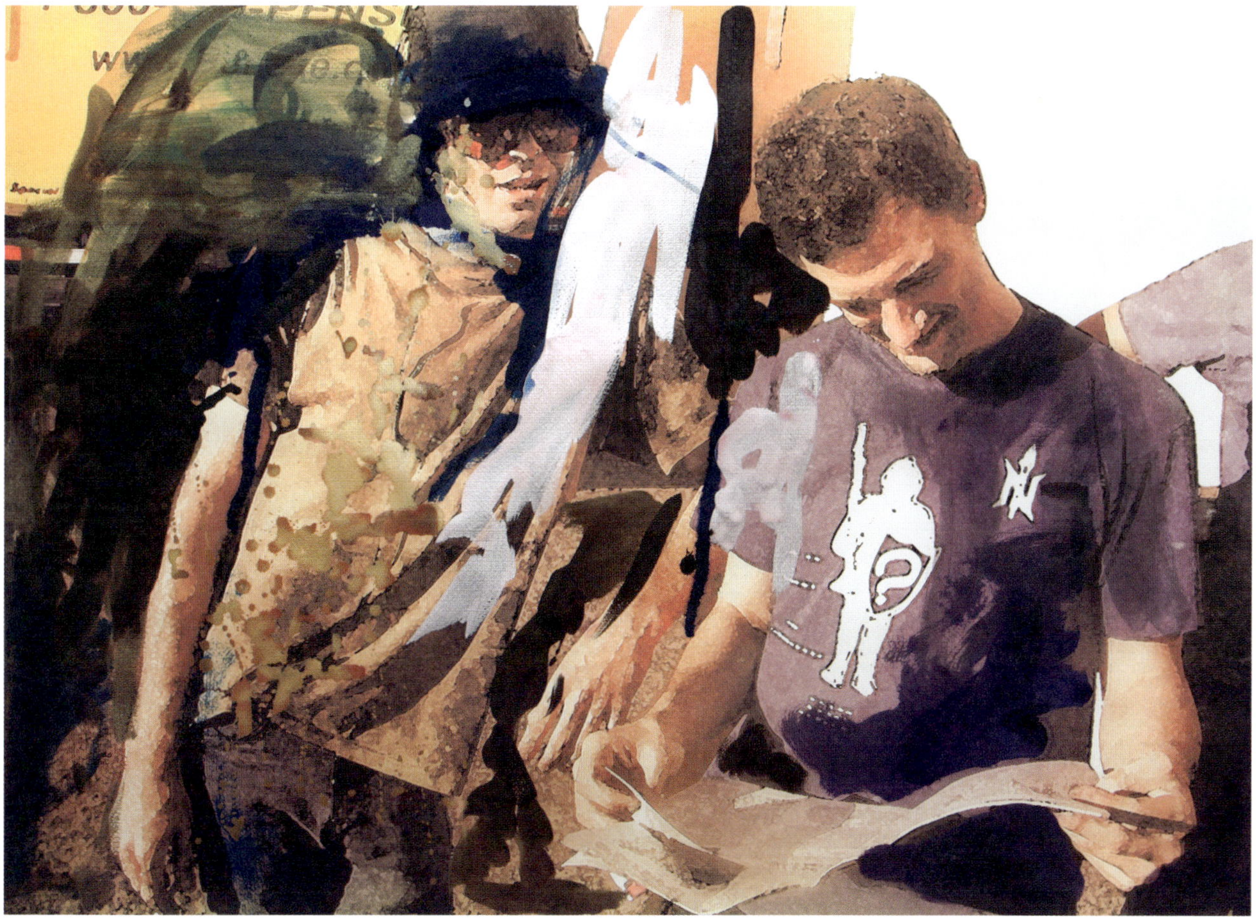

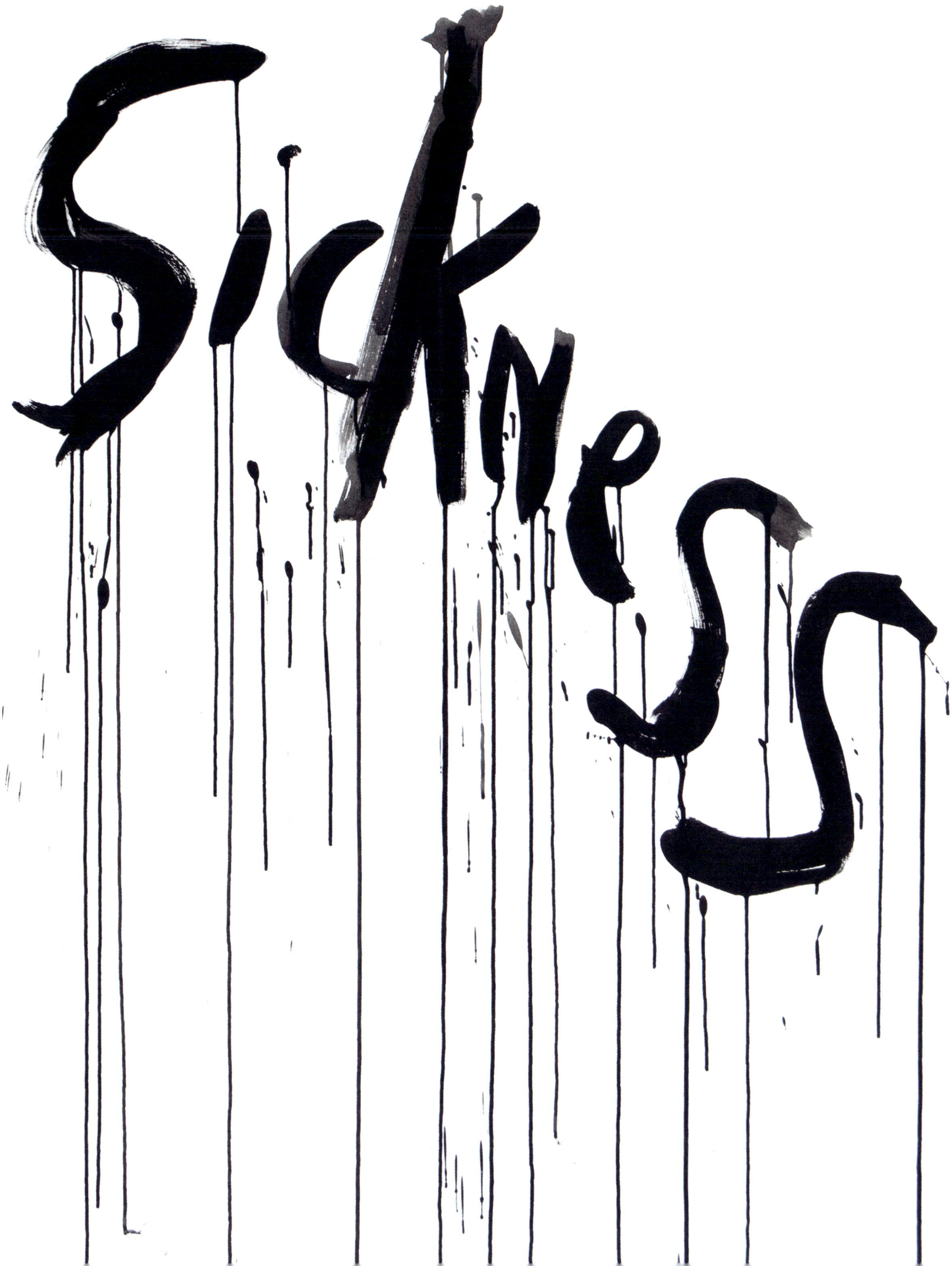
Sickness

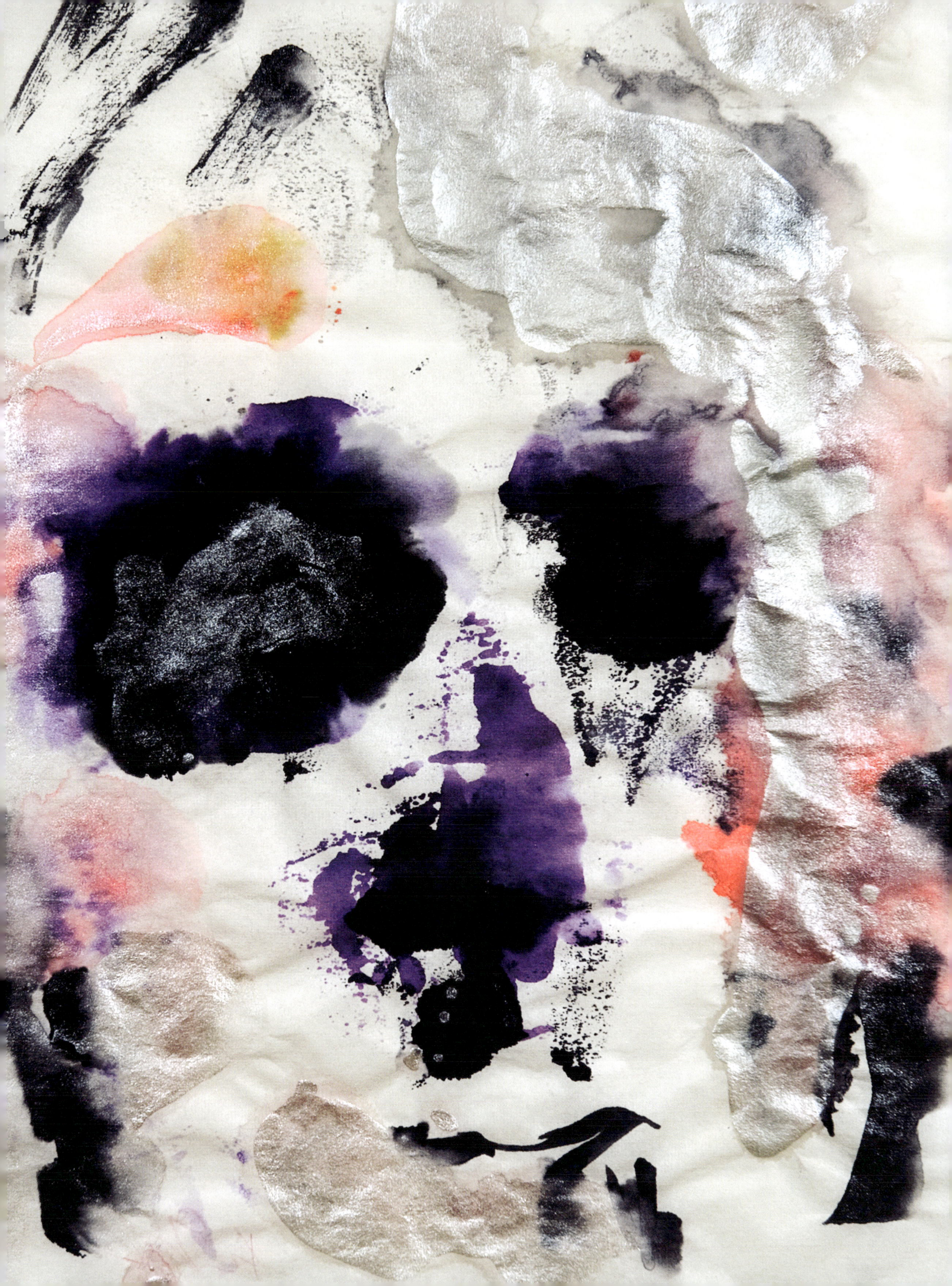

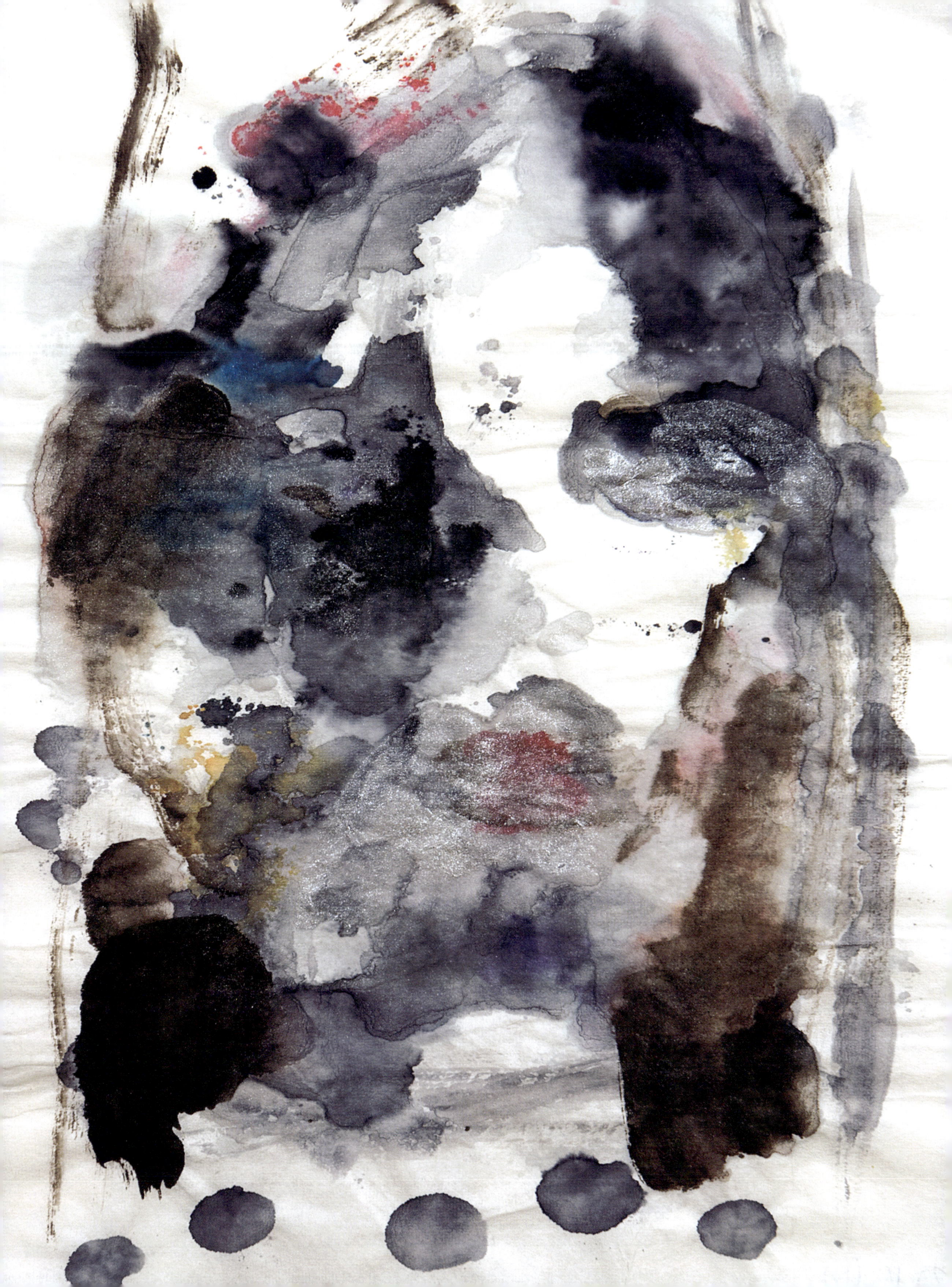

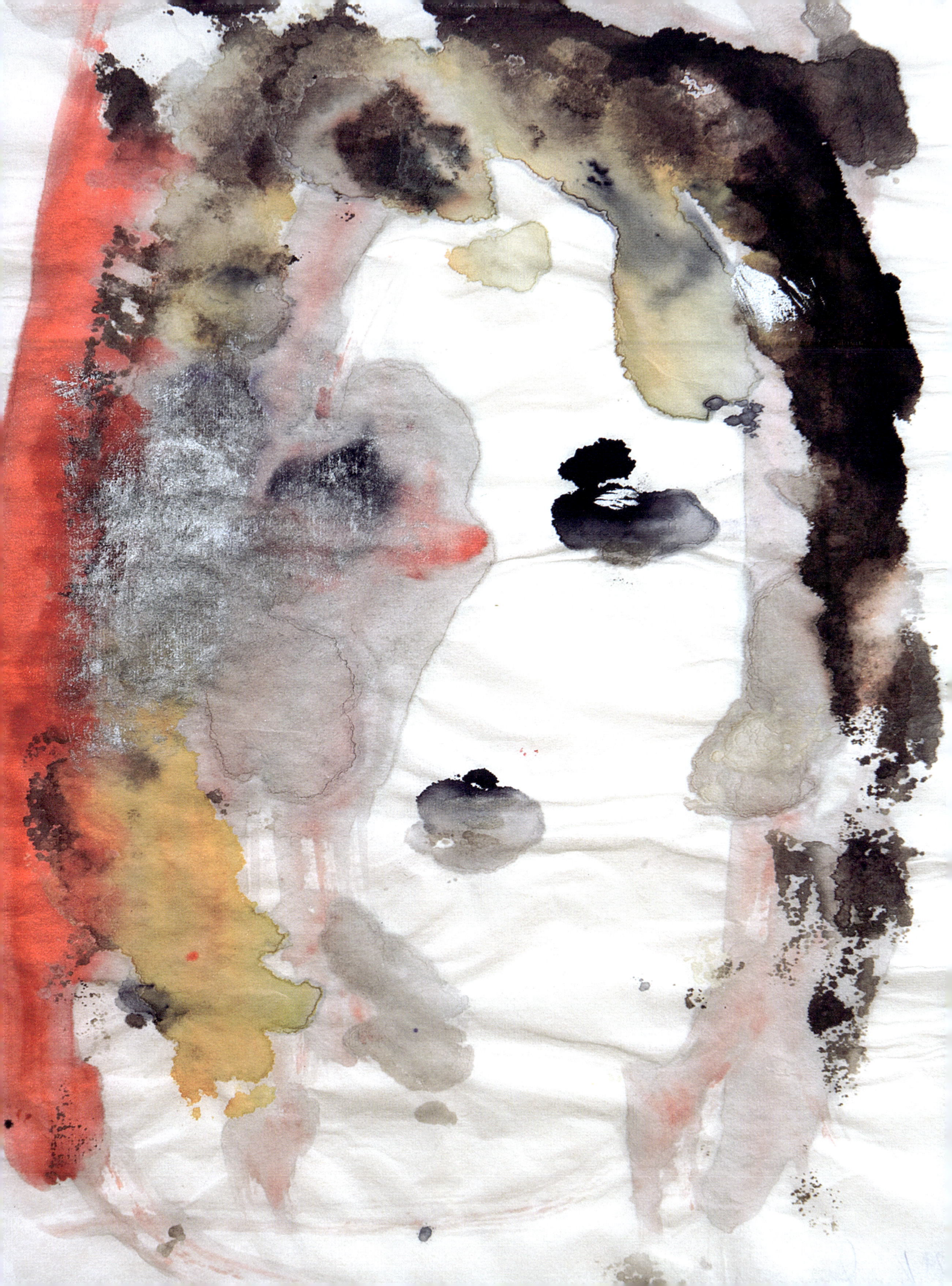

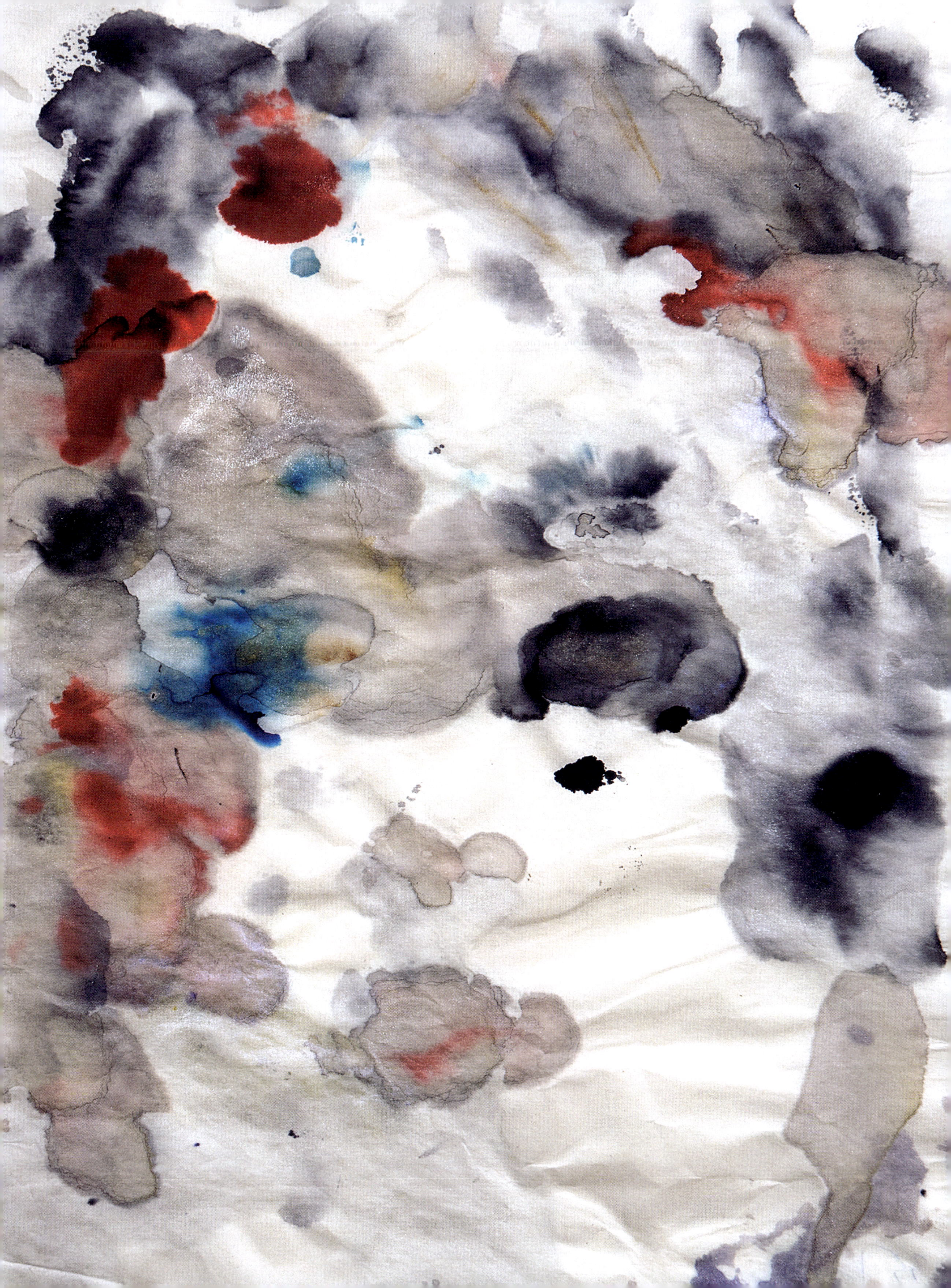

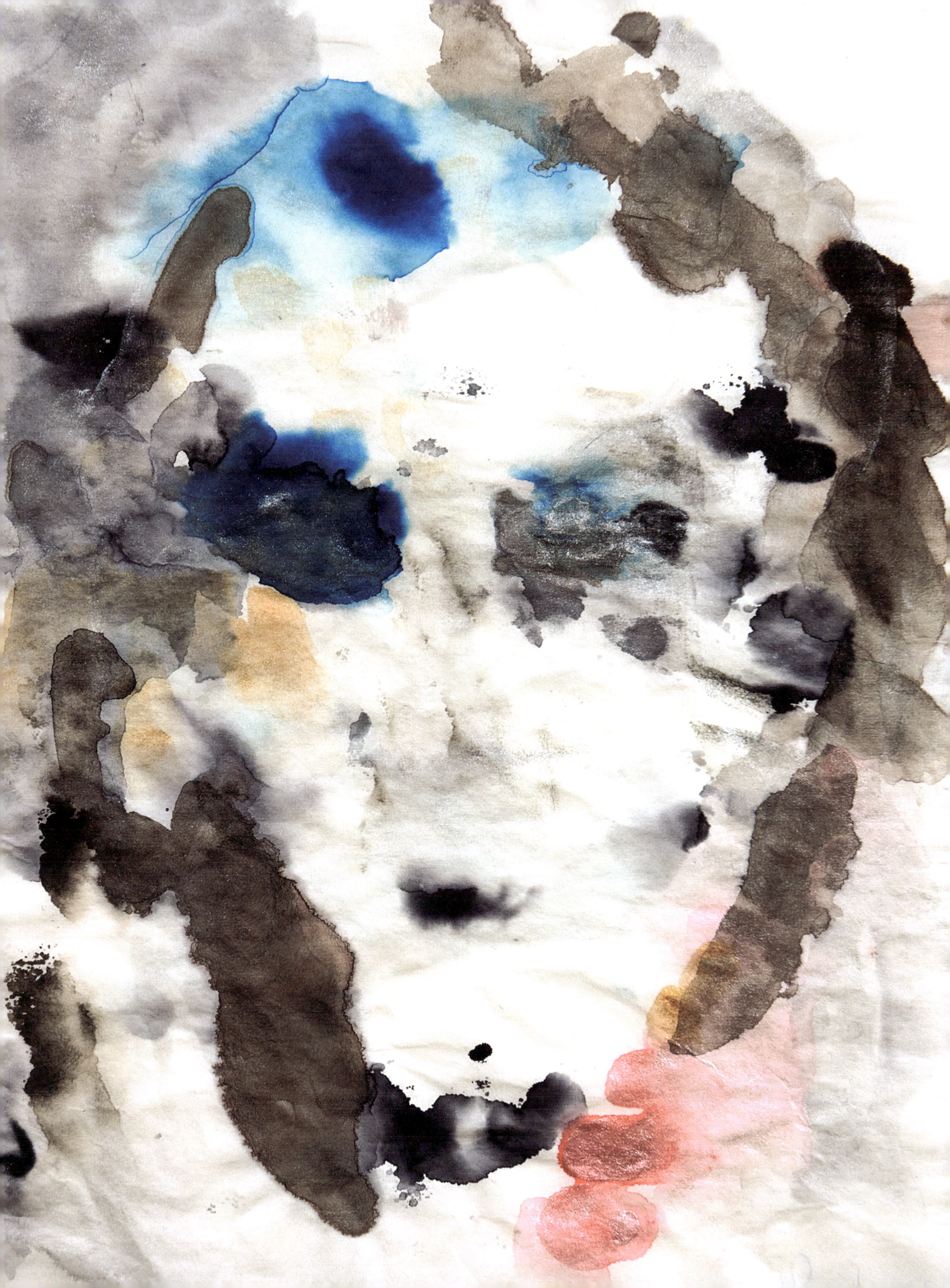

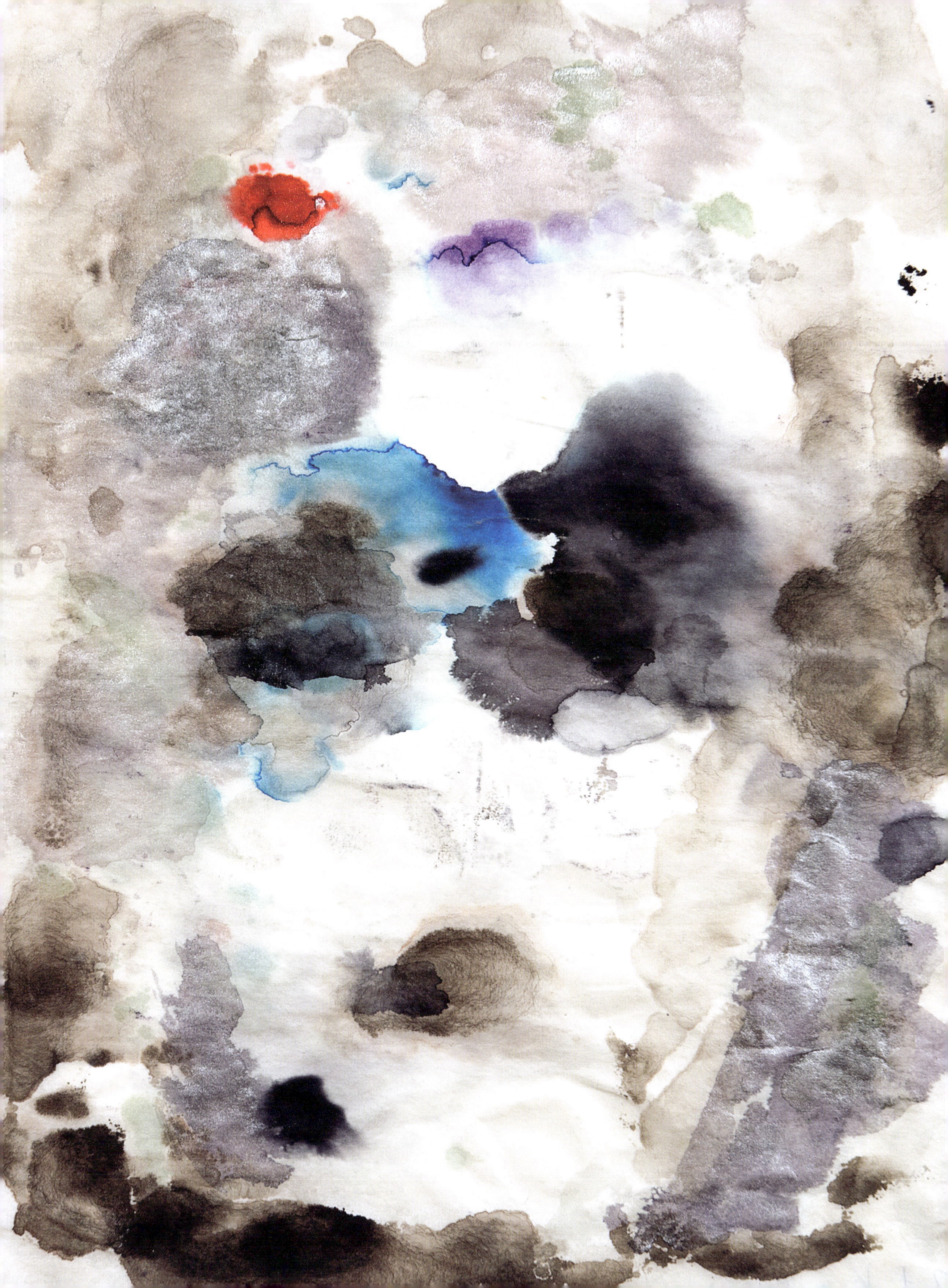

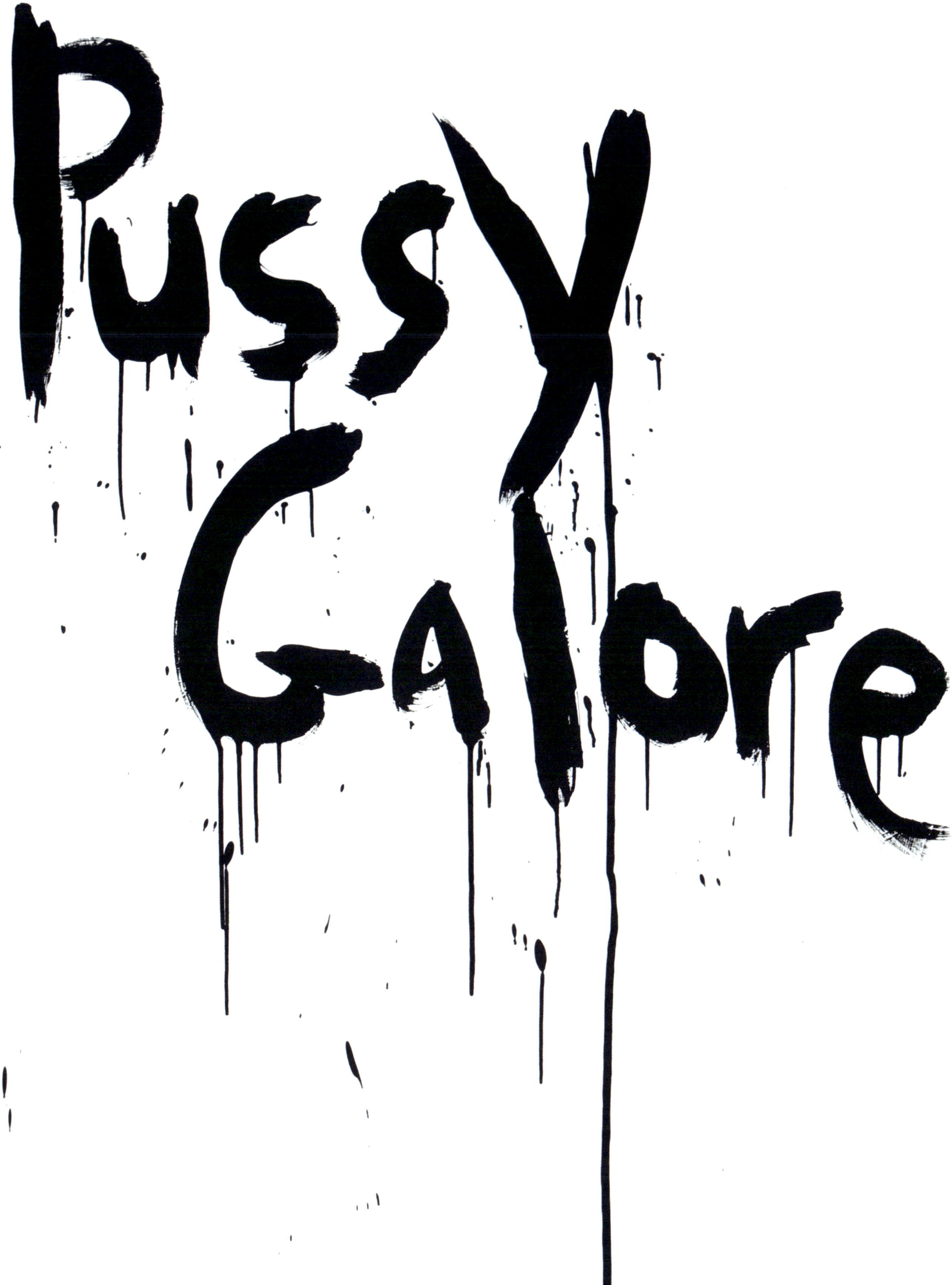
Pussy
Galore

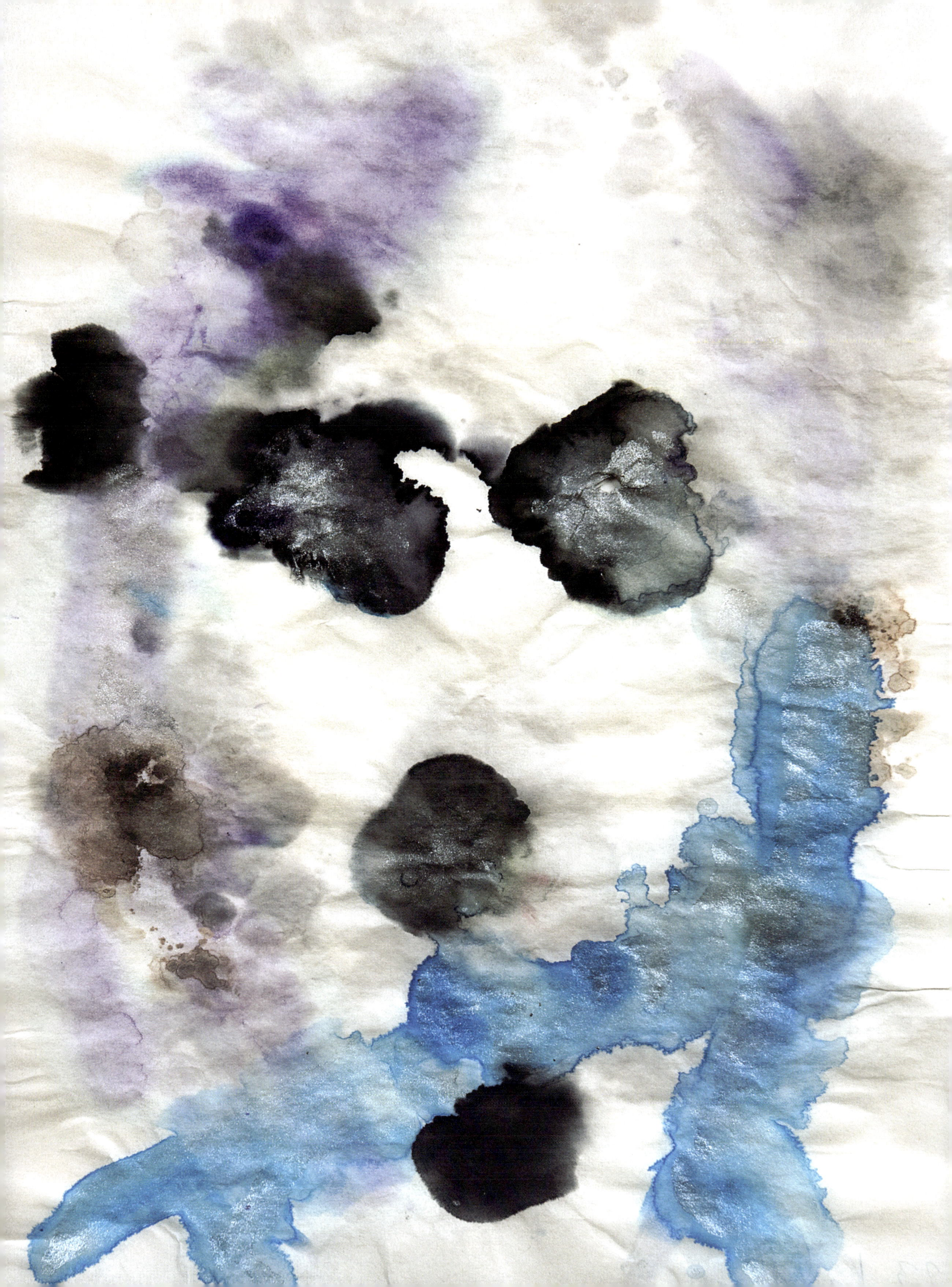

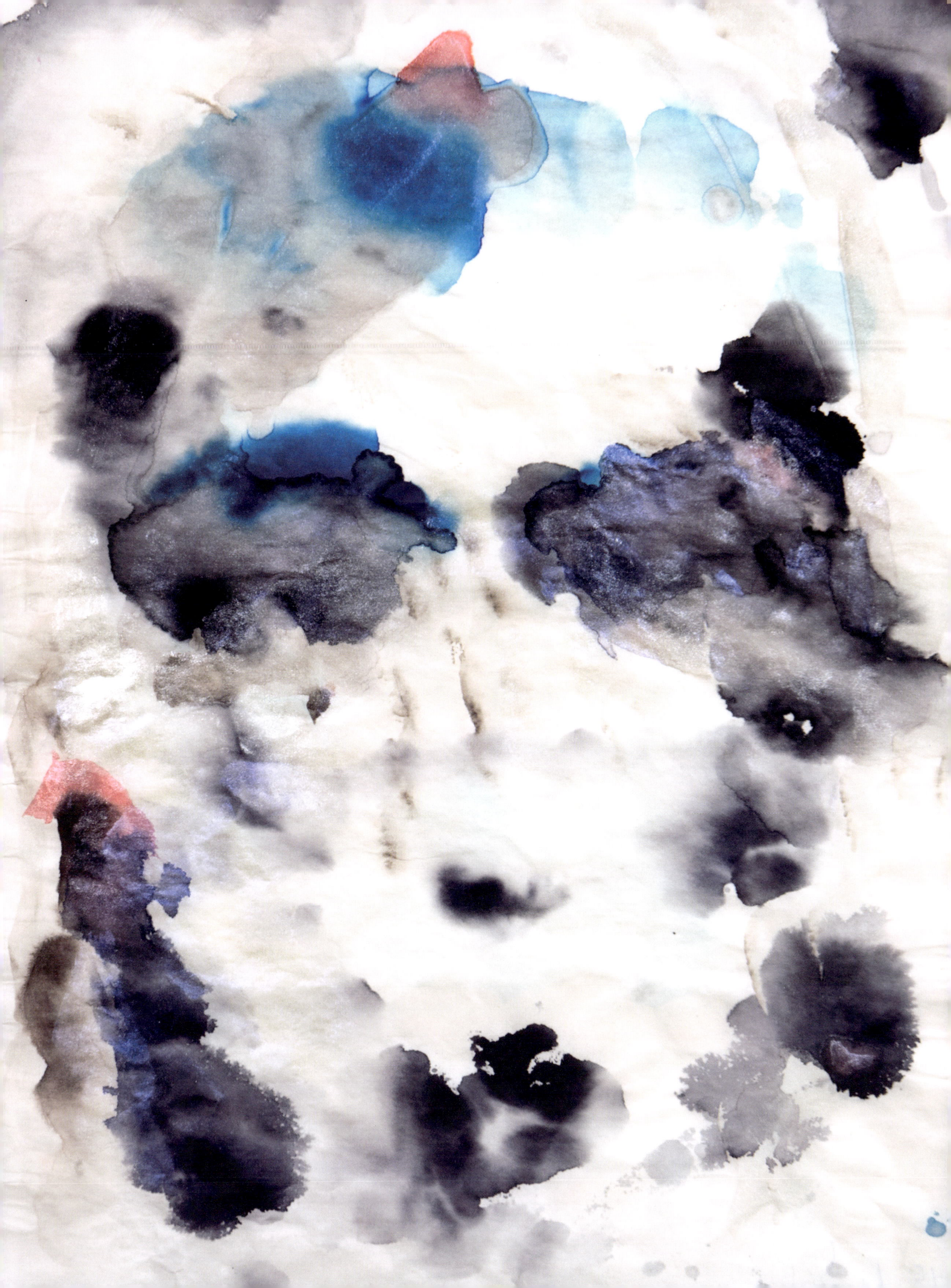

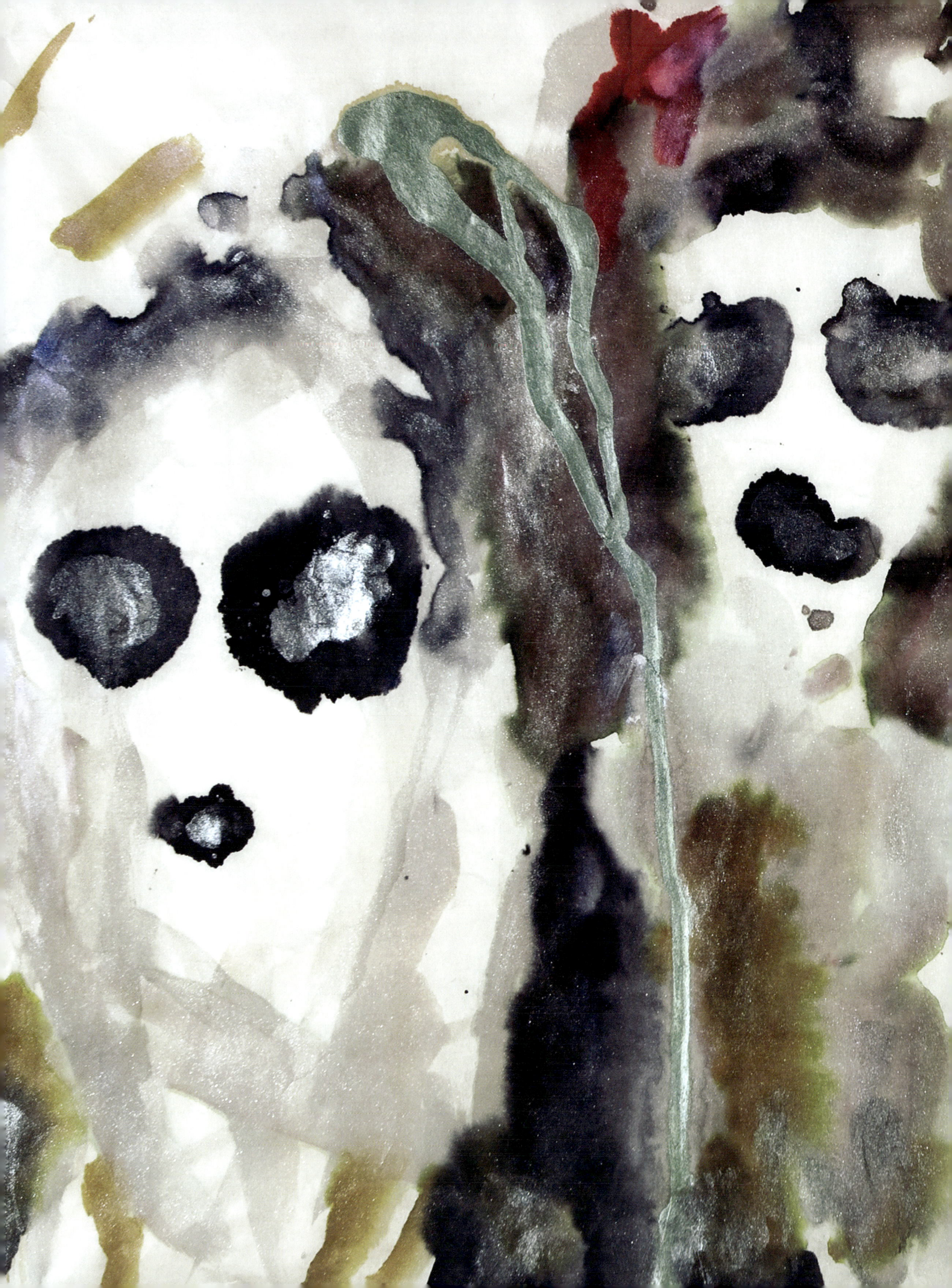

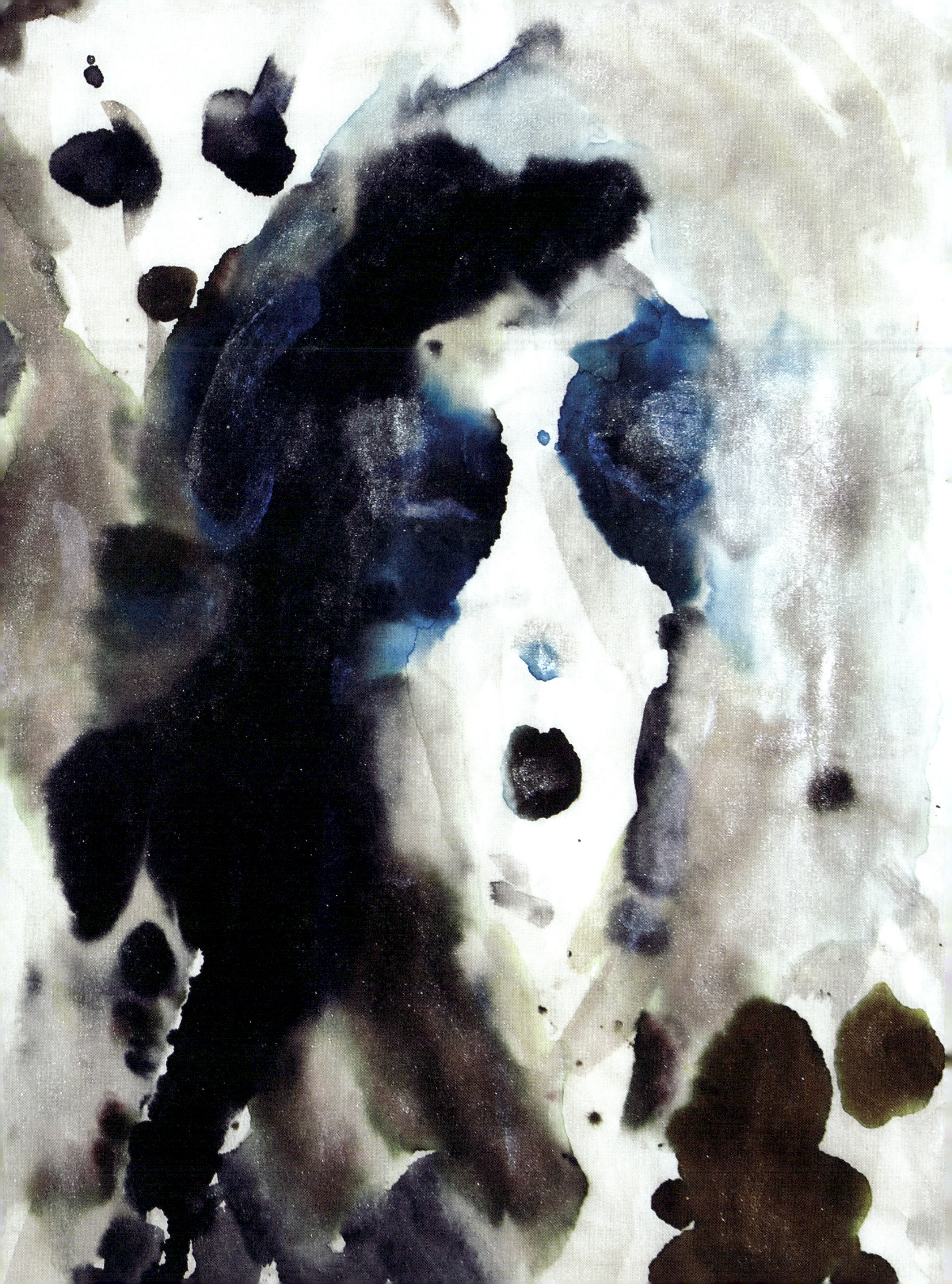

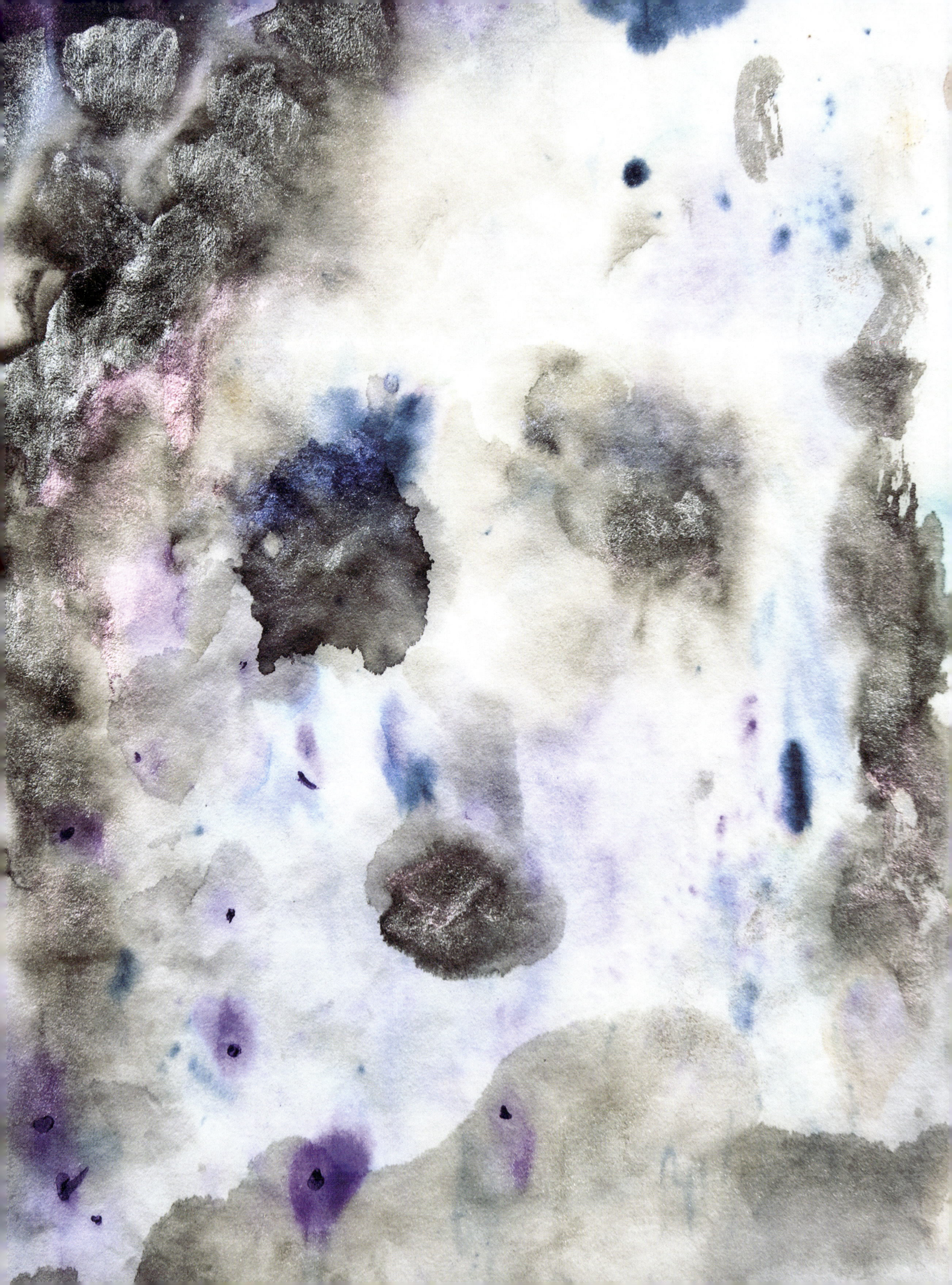

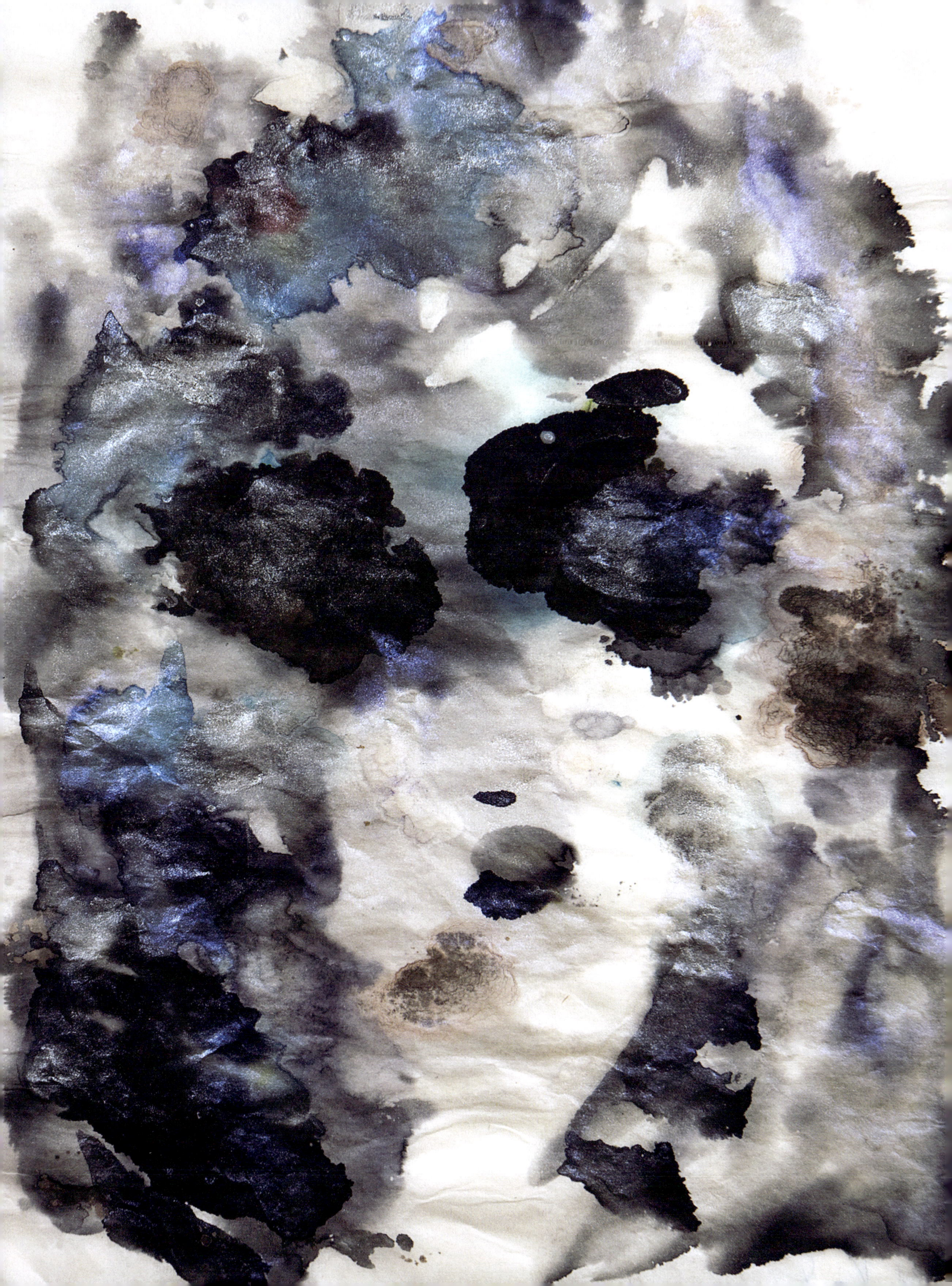

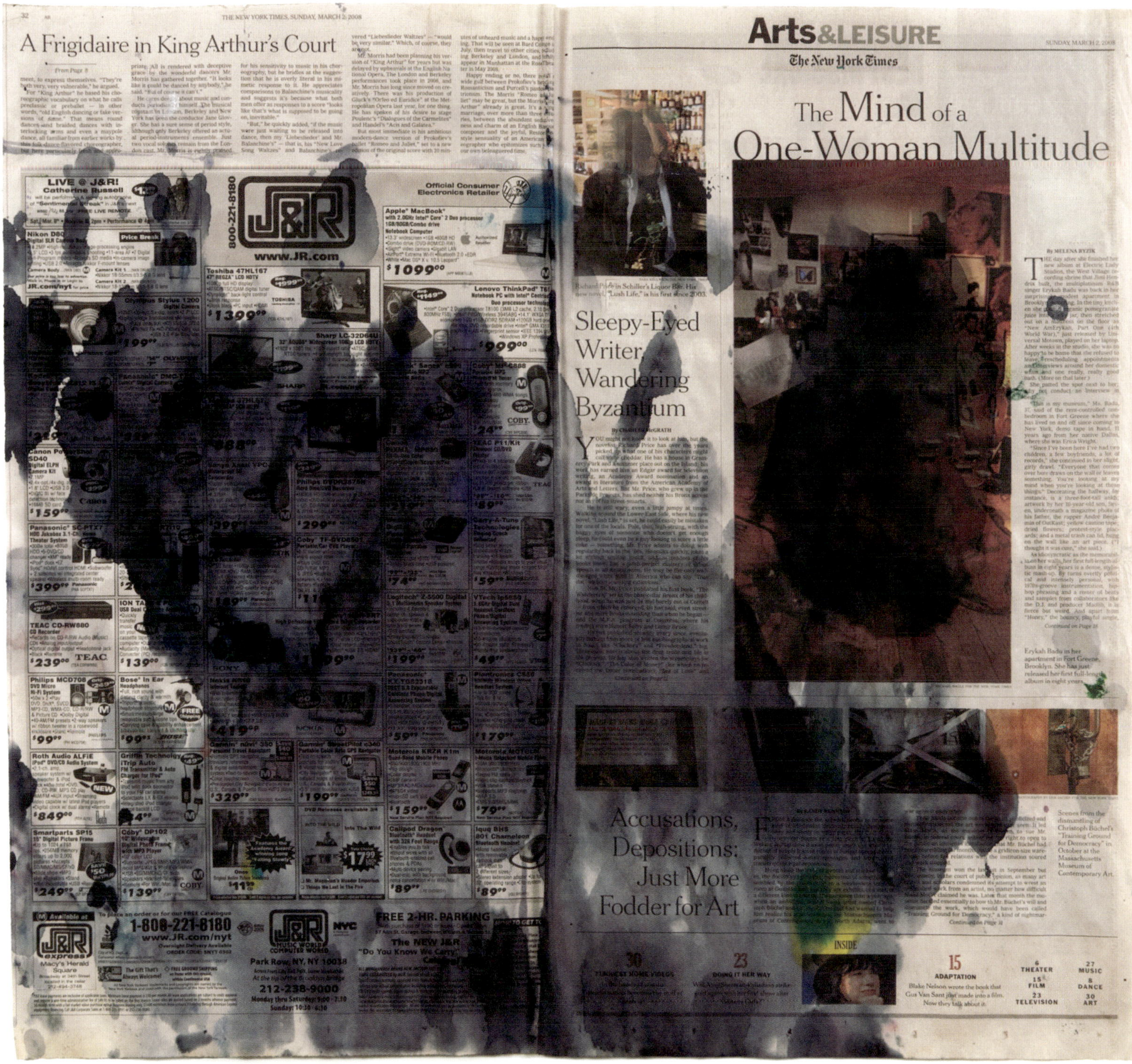
THE NEW YORK TIMES, SUNDAY, MARCH 2, 2008
A Frigidaire in King Arthur's Court
J&R
www.JR.com
800-221-8180
Official Consumer Electronics Retailer
1-800-221-8180
www.JR.com/nyt
Park Row, NY, NY 10038
212-238-9000
FREE 2-HR. PARKING
Arts&LEISURE
The New York Times
The Mind of a One-Woman Multitude
Sleepy-Eyed Writer, Wandering Byzantium
Accusations, Depositions: Just More Fodder for Art
INSIDE
15
ADAPTATION
Blake Nelson wrote the book that Gus Van Sant just made into a film. Now they talk about it.
6 THEATER
15 FILM
23 TELEVISION
27 MUSIC
8 DANCE
30 ART

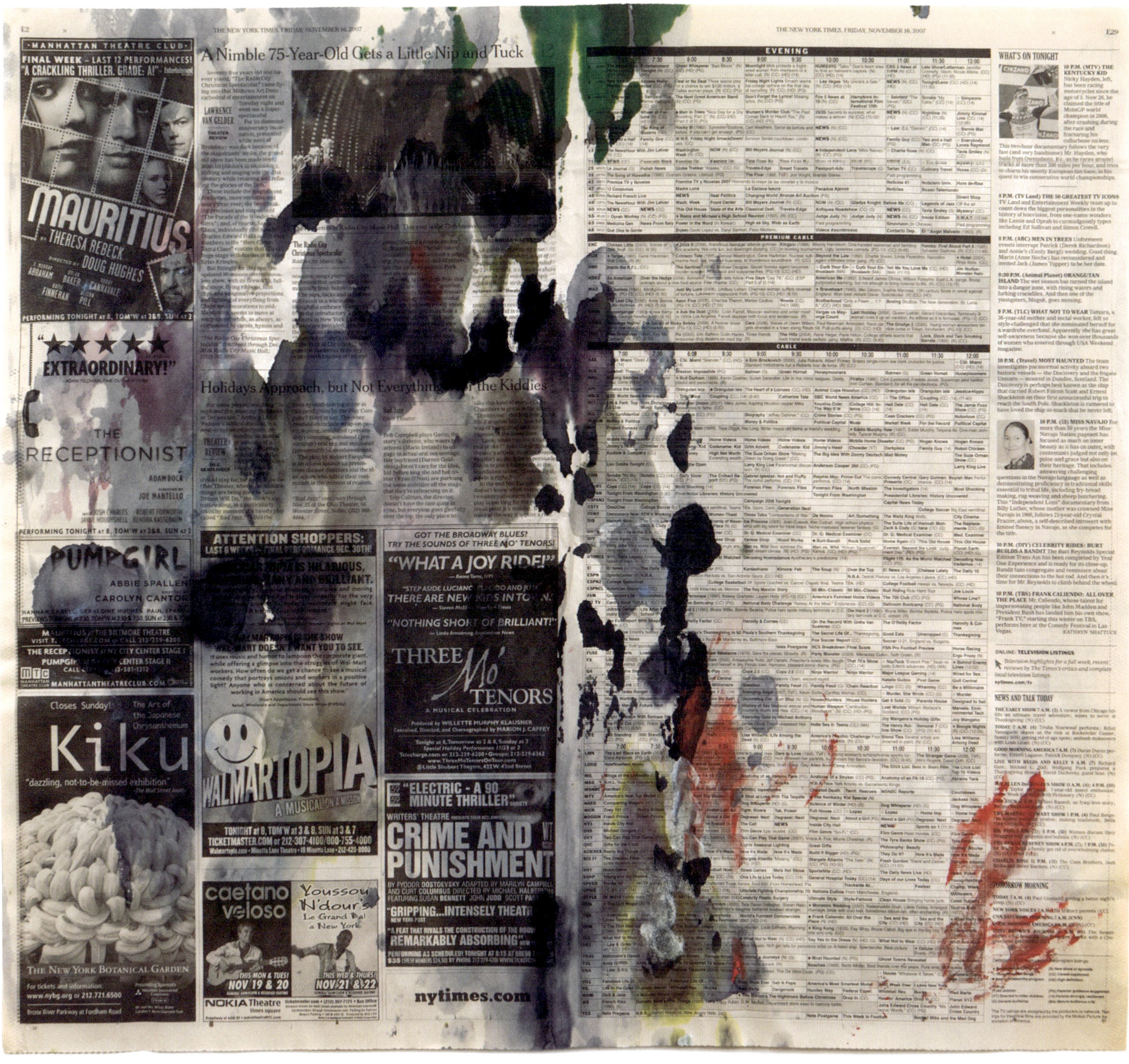
THE NEW YORK TIMES, FRIDAY, NOVEMBER 16, 2007
A Nimble 75-Year-Old Gets a Little Nip and Tuck
Holidays Approach, but Not Everything
MANHATTAN THEATRE CLUB
MAURITIUS
THERESA REBECK
DOUG HUGHES
EXTRAORDINARY!
THE RECEPTIONIST
PUMPGIRL
ATTENTION SHOPPERS:
GOT THE BROADWAY BLUES? TRY THE SOUNDS OF THREE MO' TENORS!
"WHAT A JOY RIDE!"
"NOTHING SHORT OF BRILLIANT!"
THREE Mó TENORS
Kiku
THE NEW YORK BOTANICAL GARDEN
WALMARTOPIA
"ELECTRIC - A 90 MINUTE THRILLER"
CRIME AND PUNISHMENT
caetano veloso
Youssou N'dour's
NOKIA Theatre
nytimes.com
EVENING
PREMIUM CABLE
CABLE
WHAT'S ON TONIGHT
NEWS AND TALK TODAY
TOMORROW MORNING

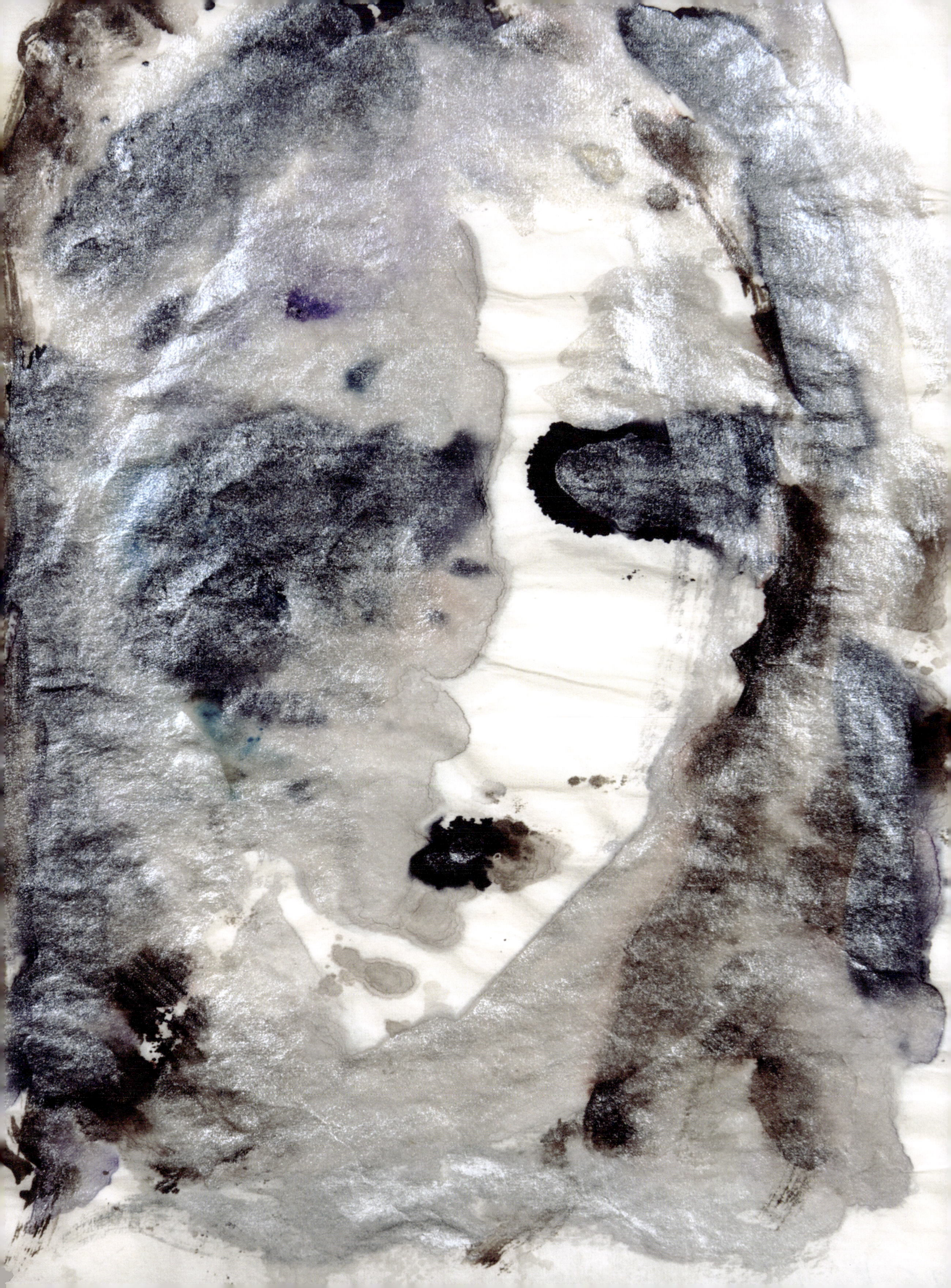

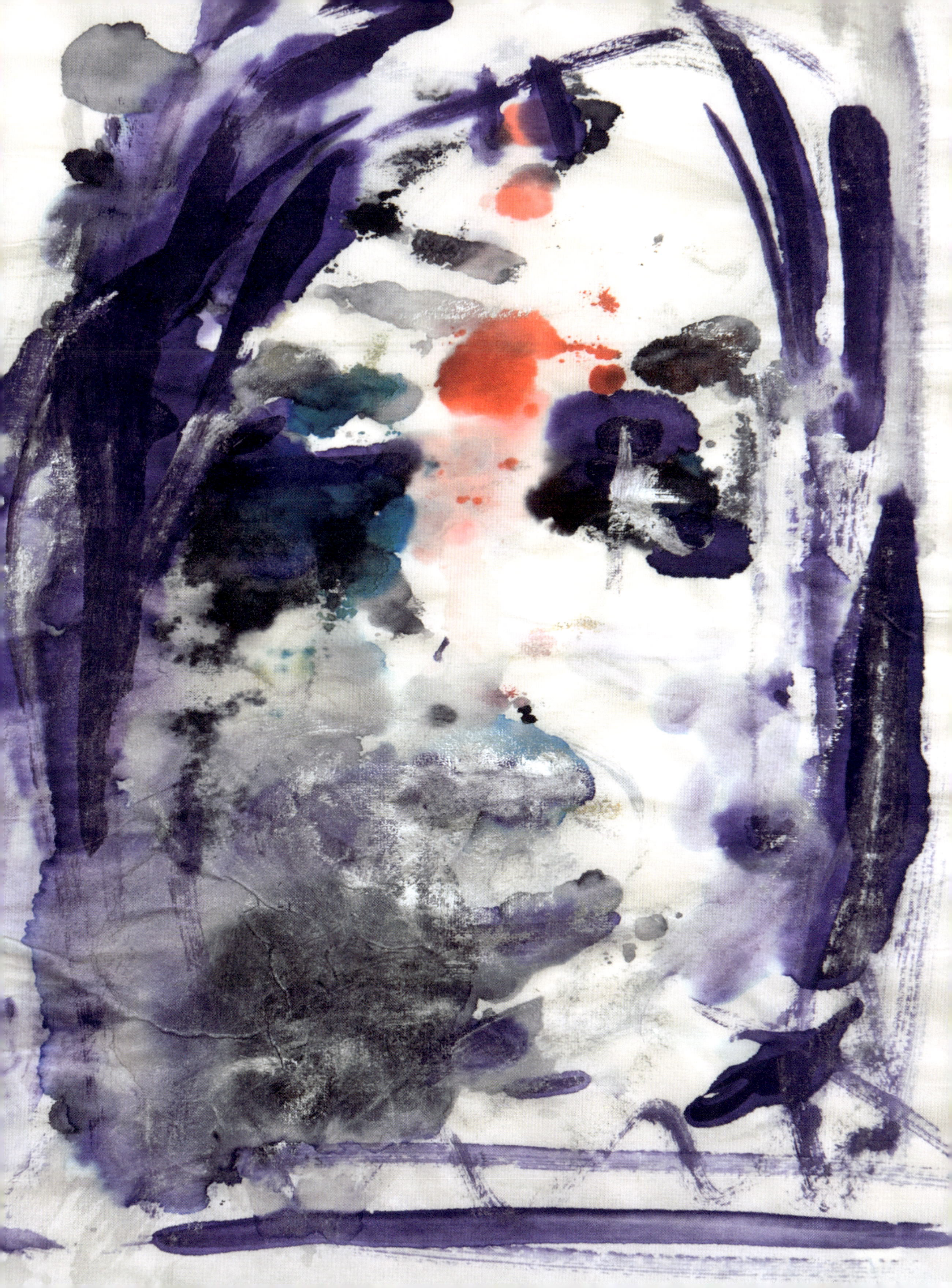

As he bent toward the amp to turn it up his hair fell over his eye his fingers touched the fret board he was strumming fast for a minute, then he started strumming slowing pressing his fingers on the fret moving his fingers up and down the fret board then he struck the guitar, he leaned into the amp and turned up the volume he placed the front of the guitar against the face of the amp gently he moved the guitar rubbing it on the amp then he swung the guitar forward and back keeping the neck of the guitar away from the amp he stood with his legs apart he swung his arm around like a windmill and he turned to face the audience he stopped playing suddenly he turned to look at the other musician he put his guitar down on the floor he started to lie down on the floor he was playing his guitar rolling around he took his strap off and started slapping the strap on the guitar he went over to the amp and he pulled it out and he twirled it around, the reverb sounded out he picked up the guitar and he leaned it against the amp he closed his eyes he walked away.

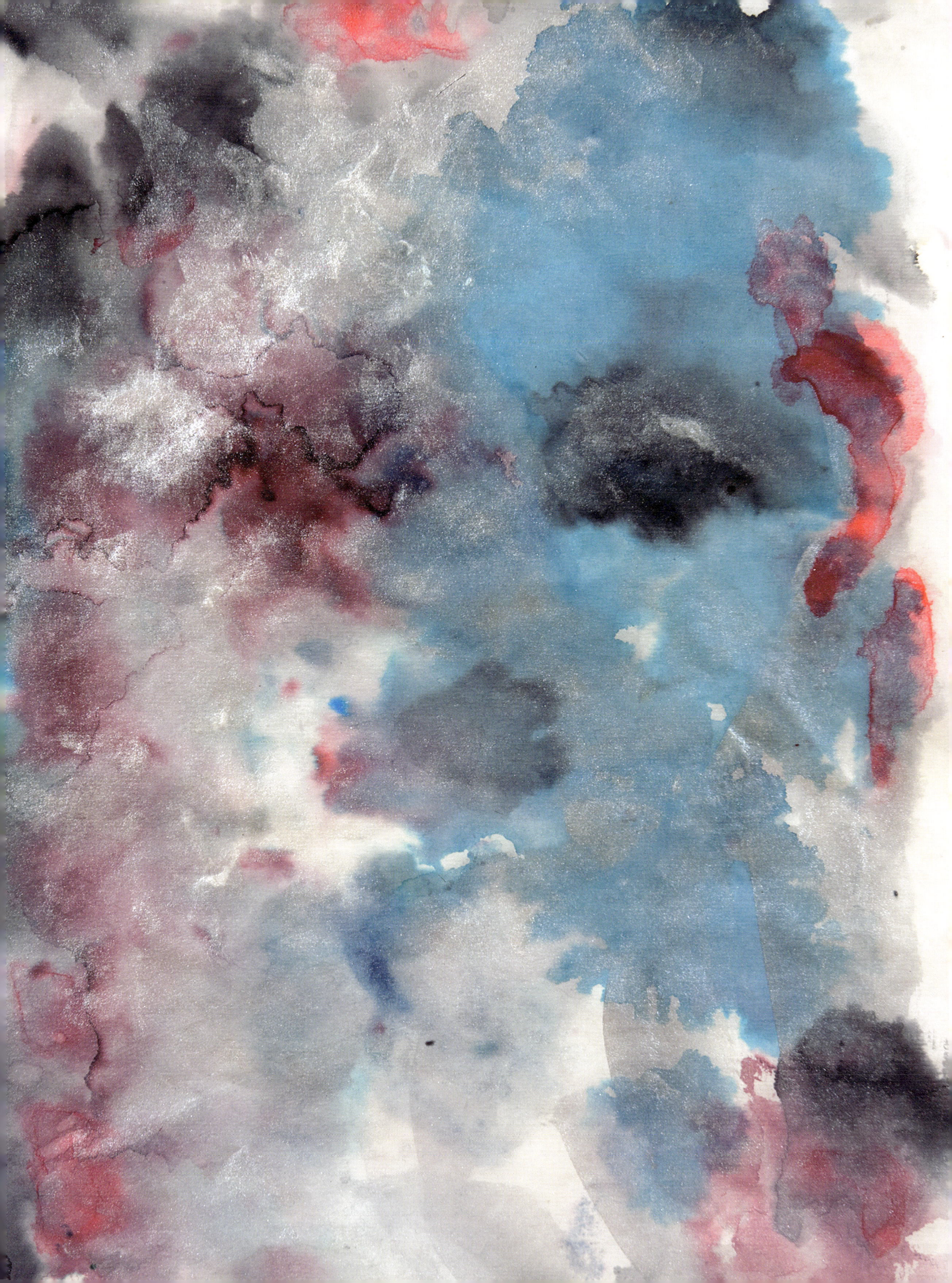

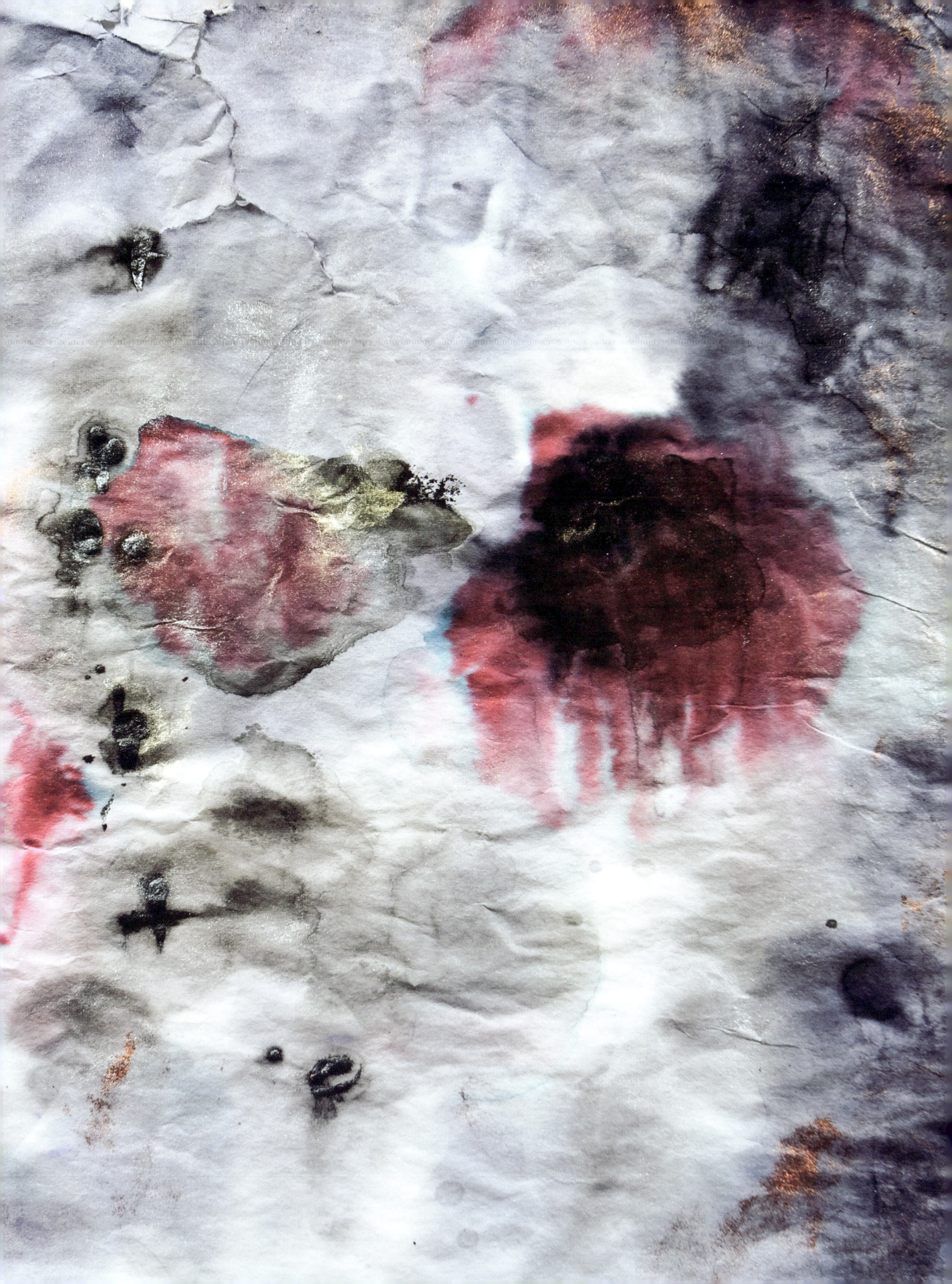

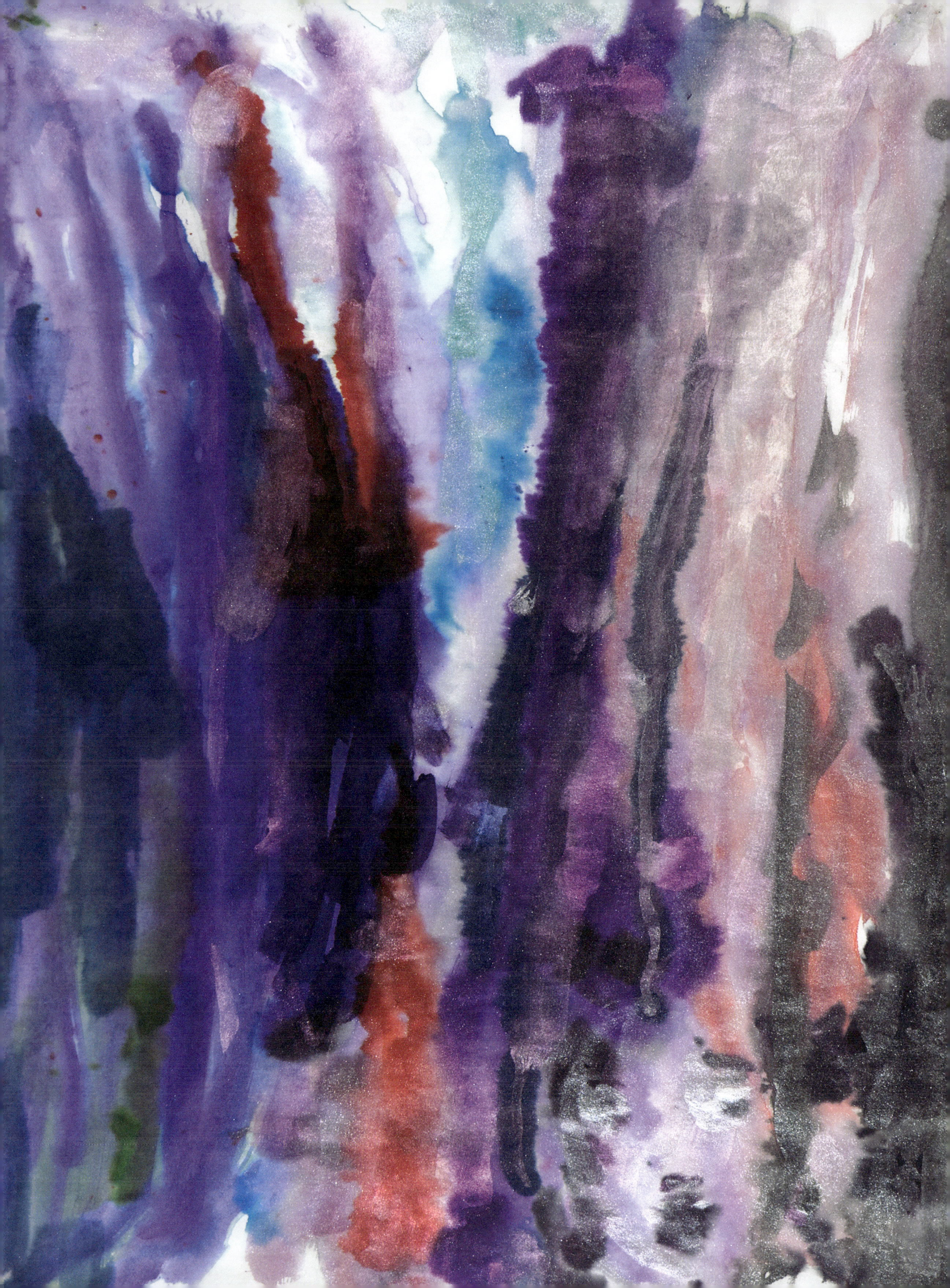

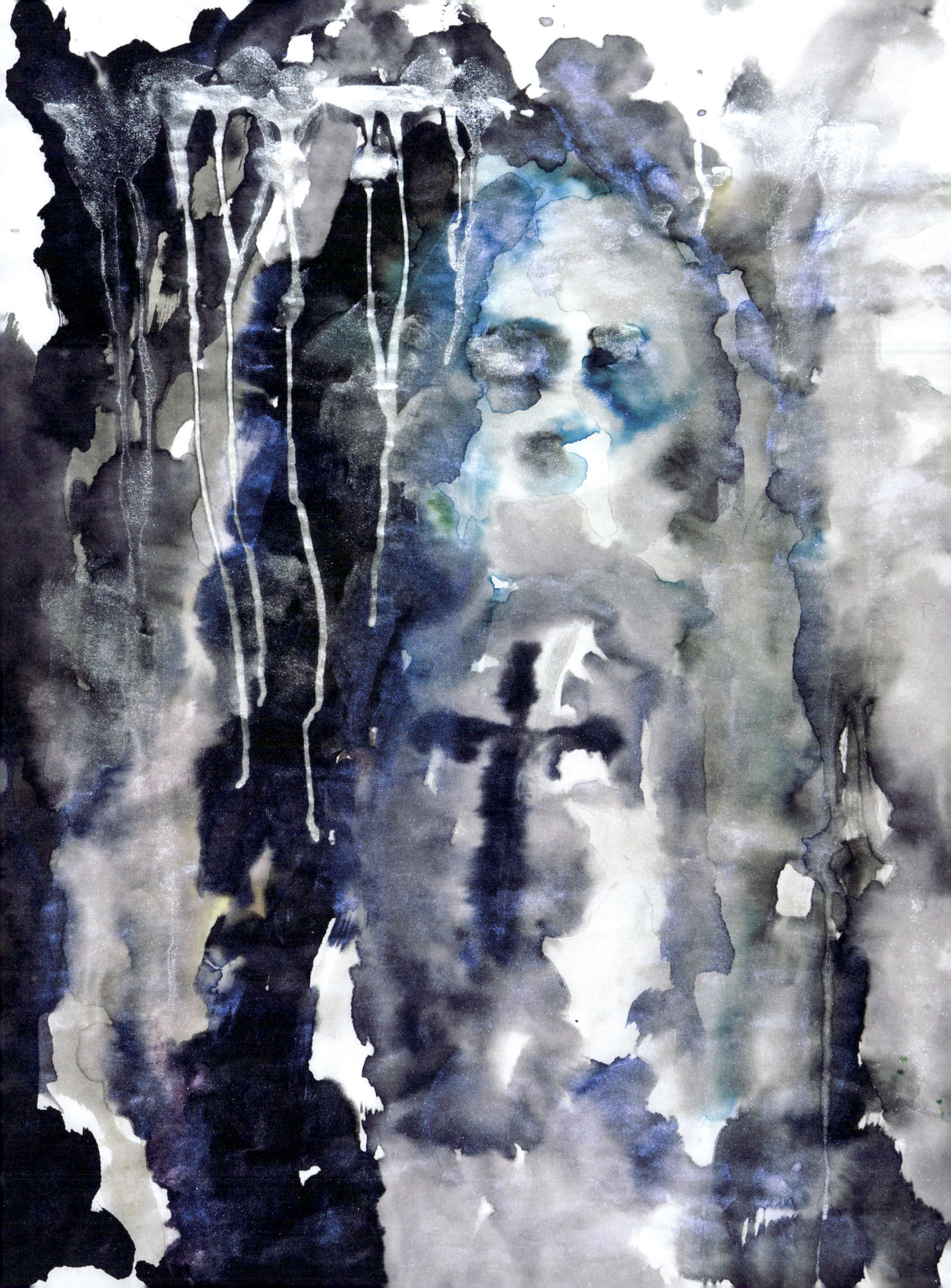

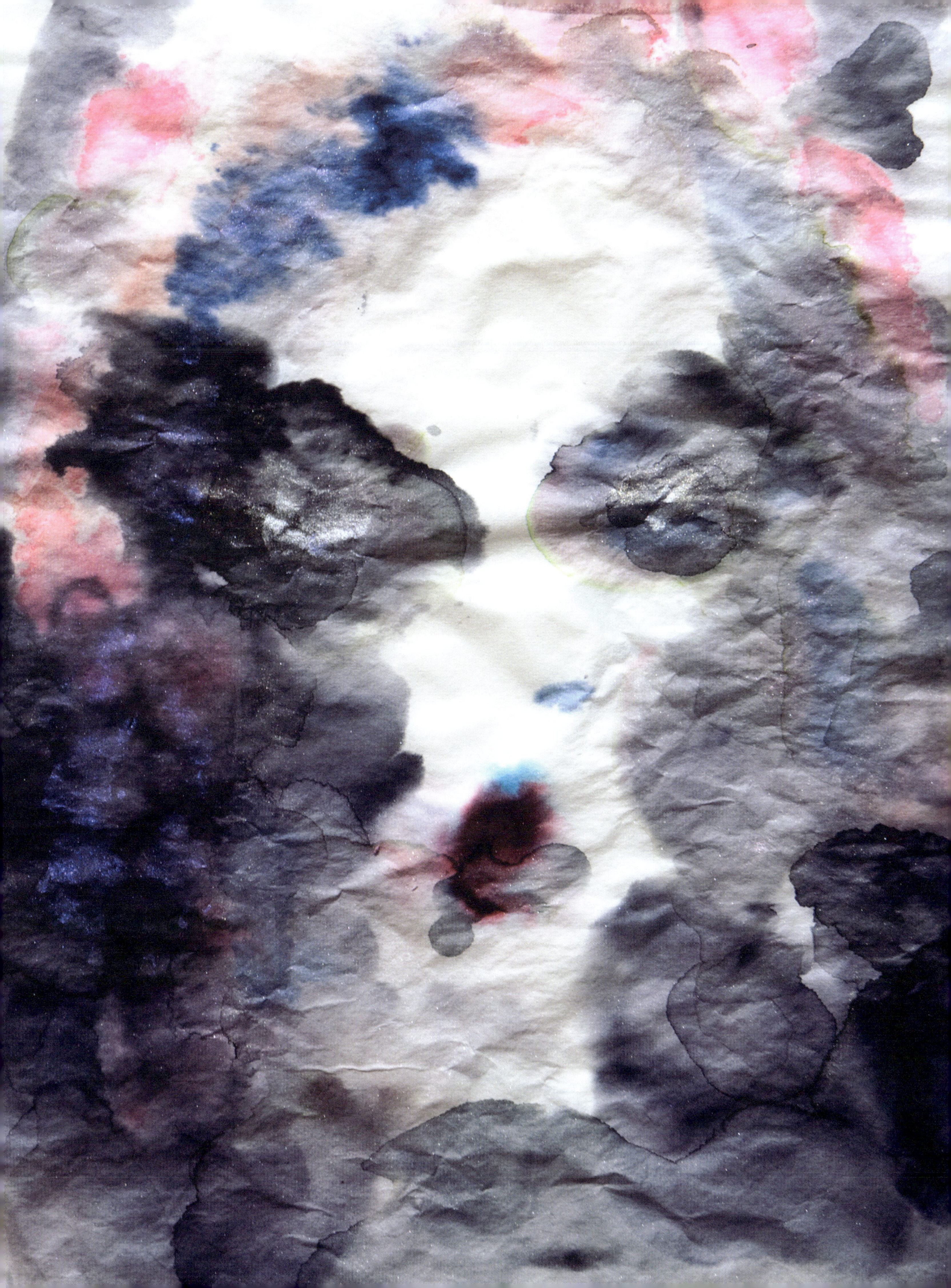

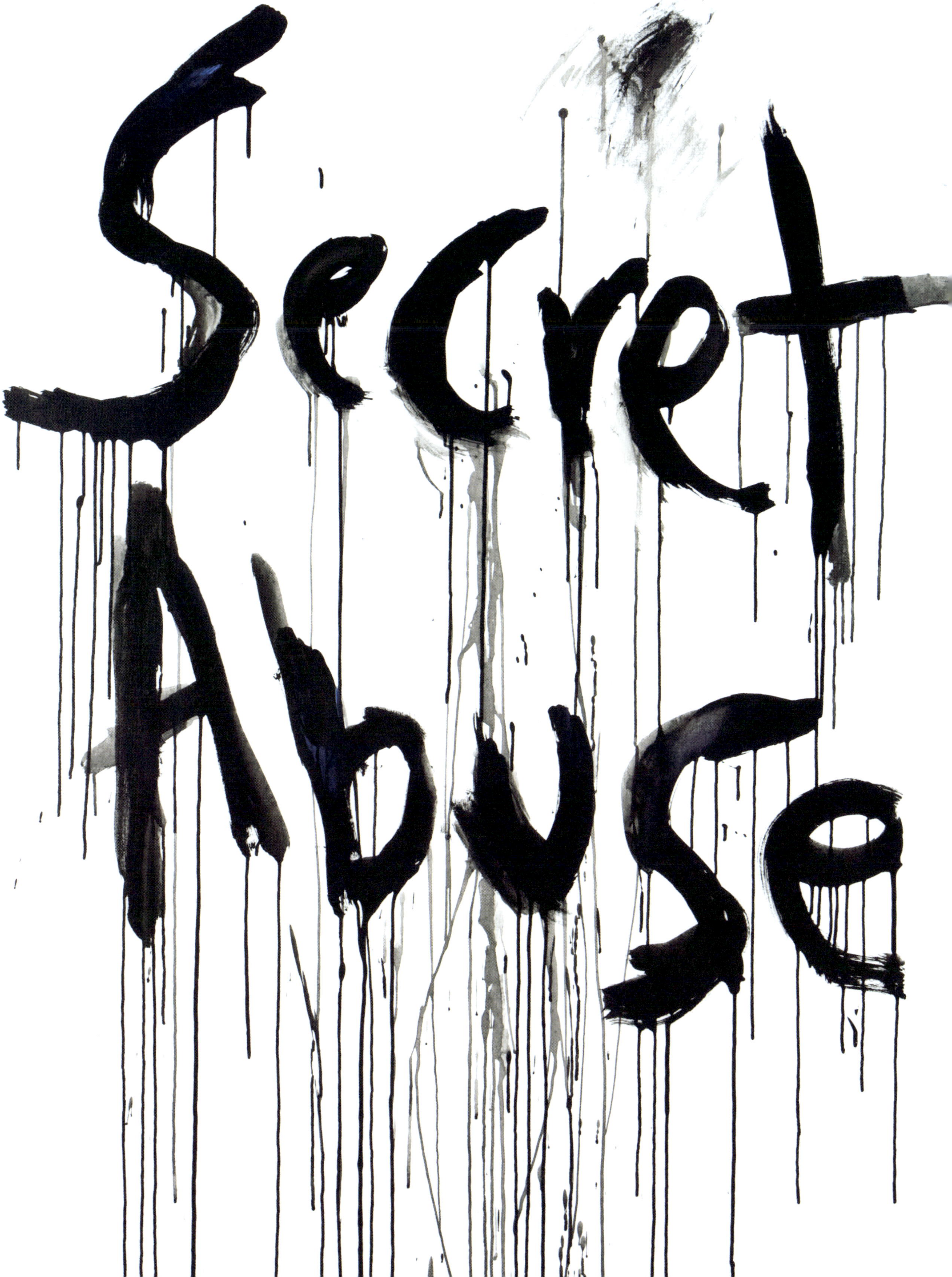
Secret
Abuse

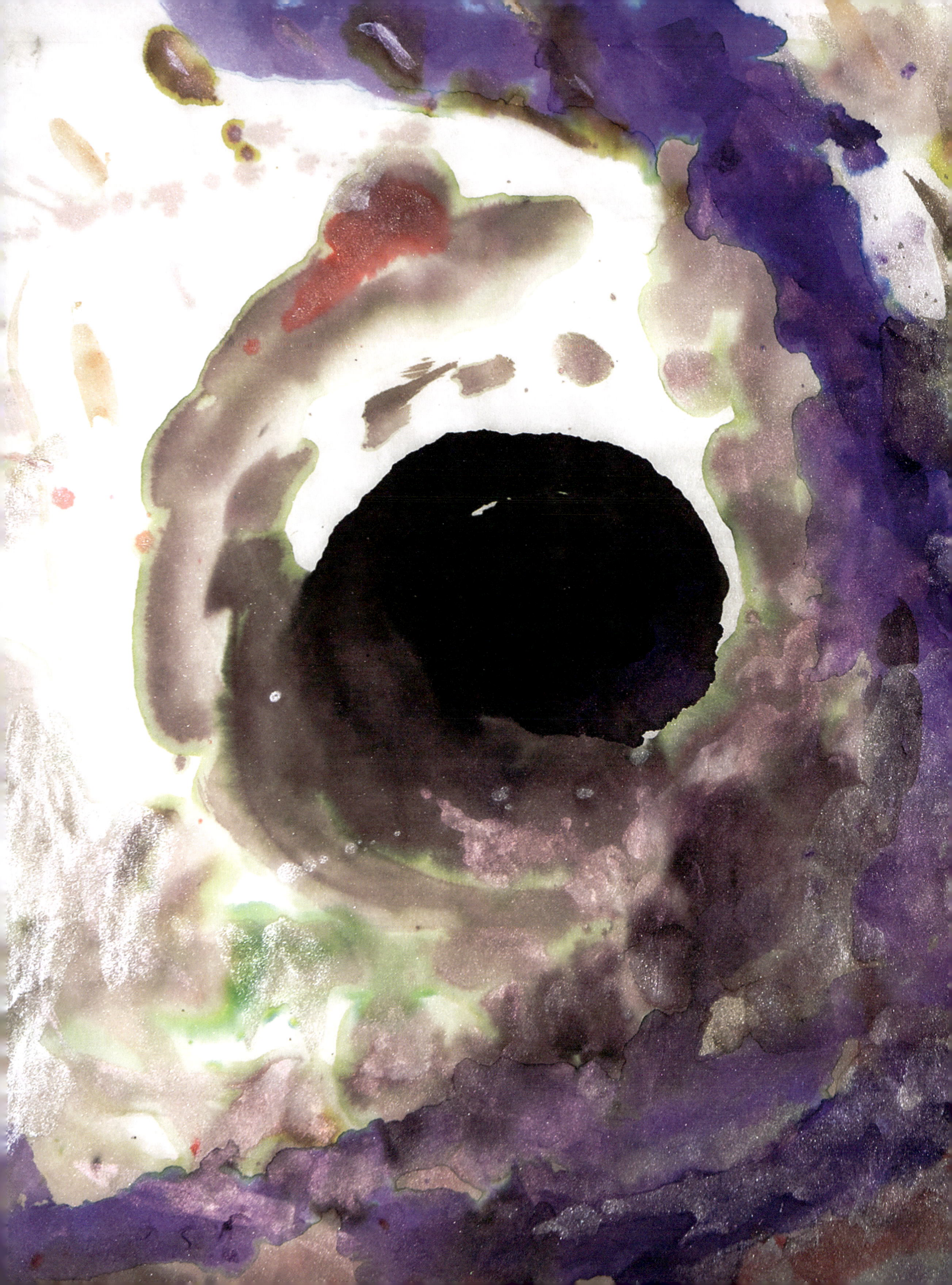

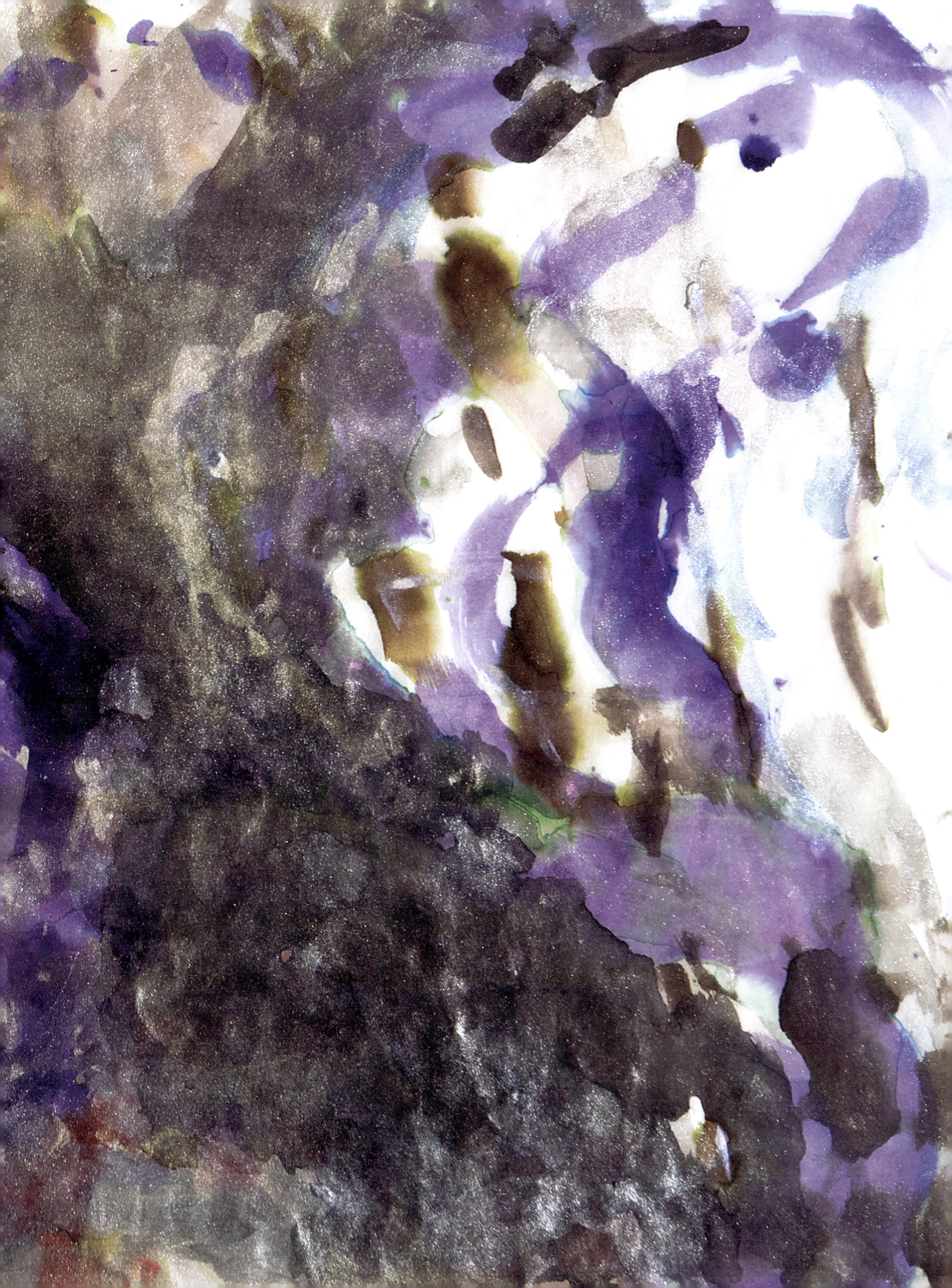

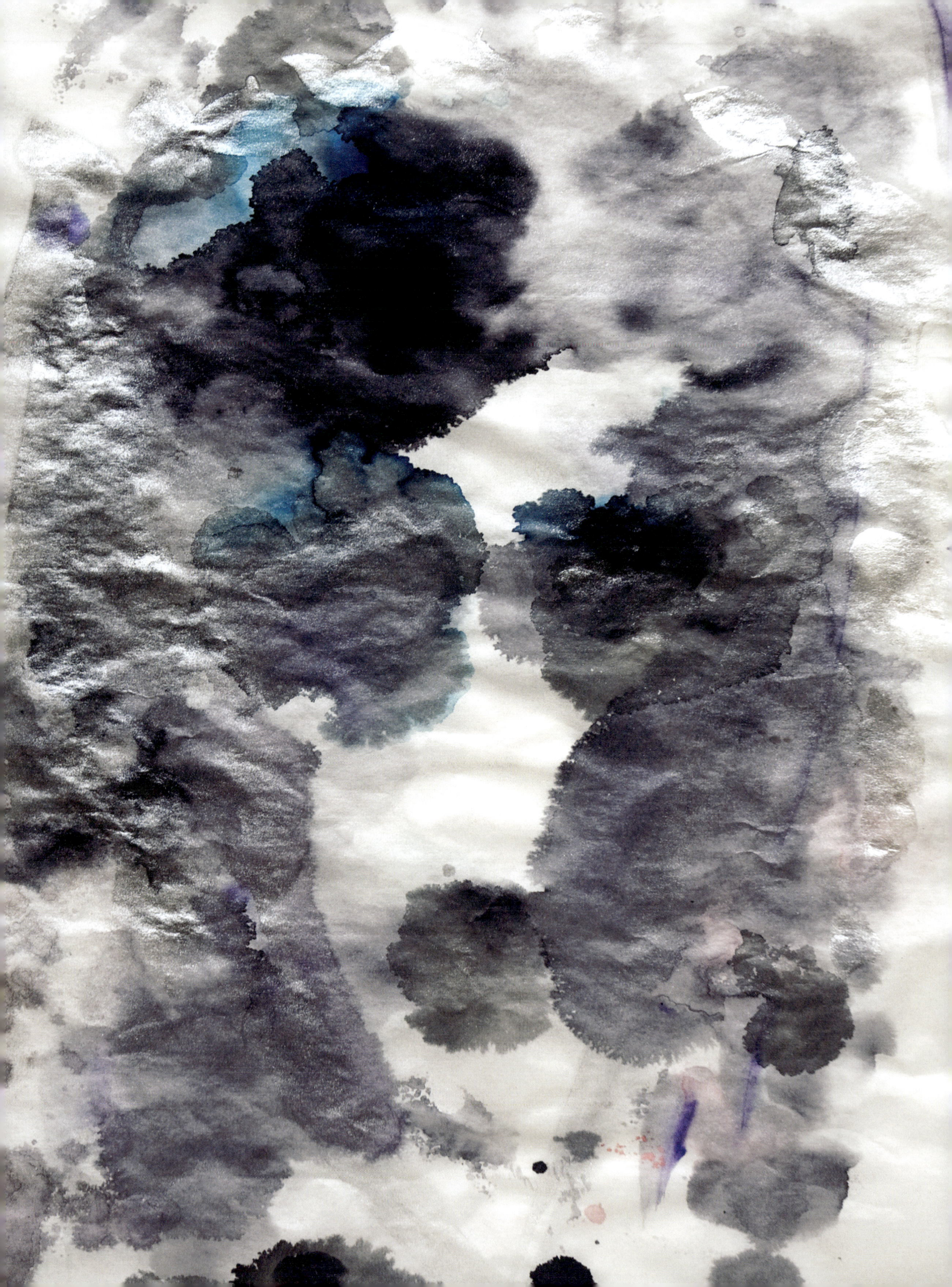

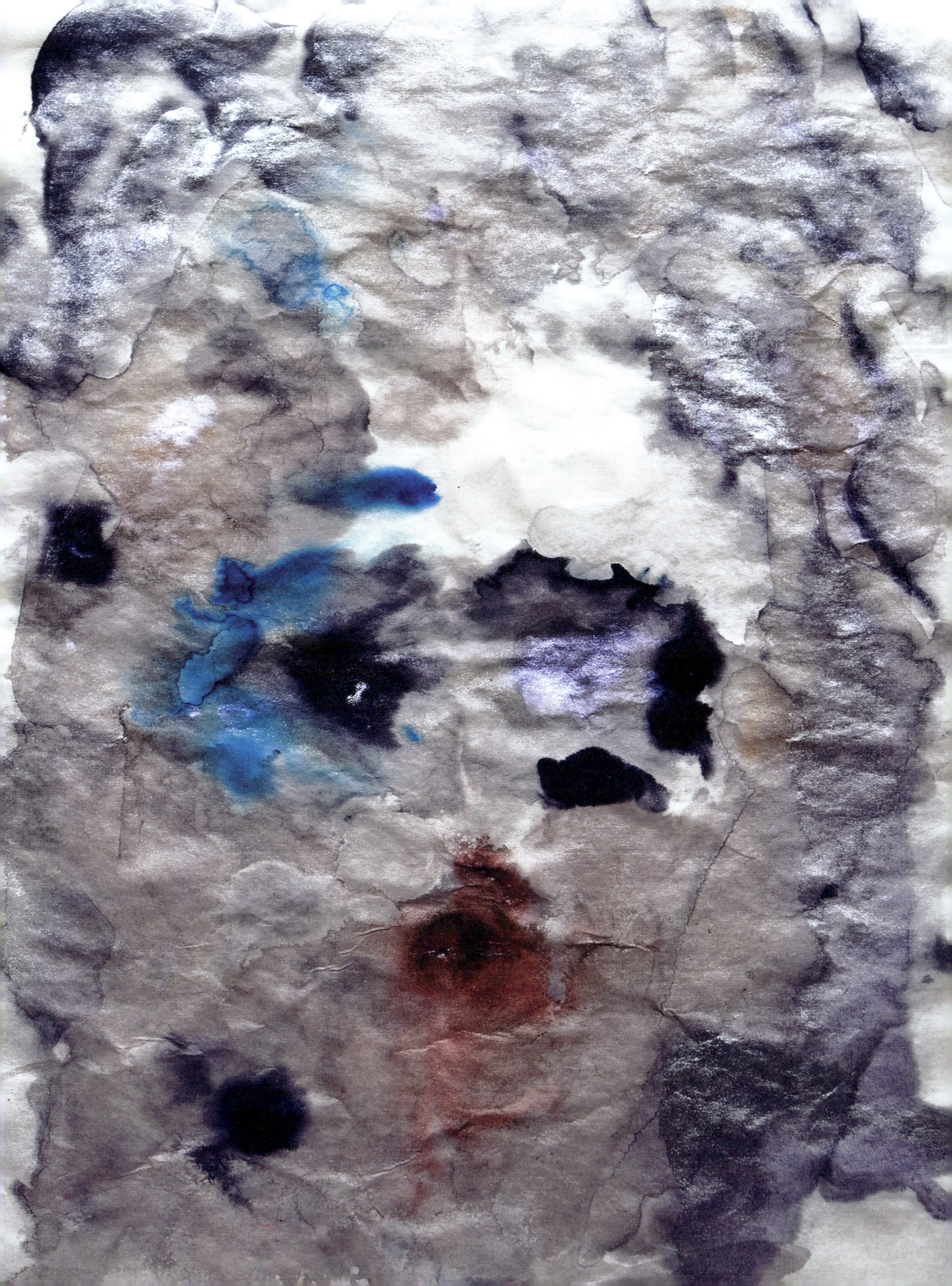

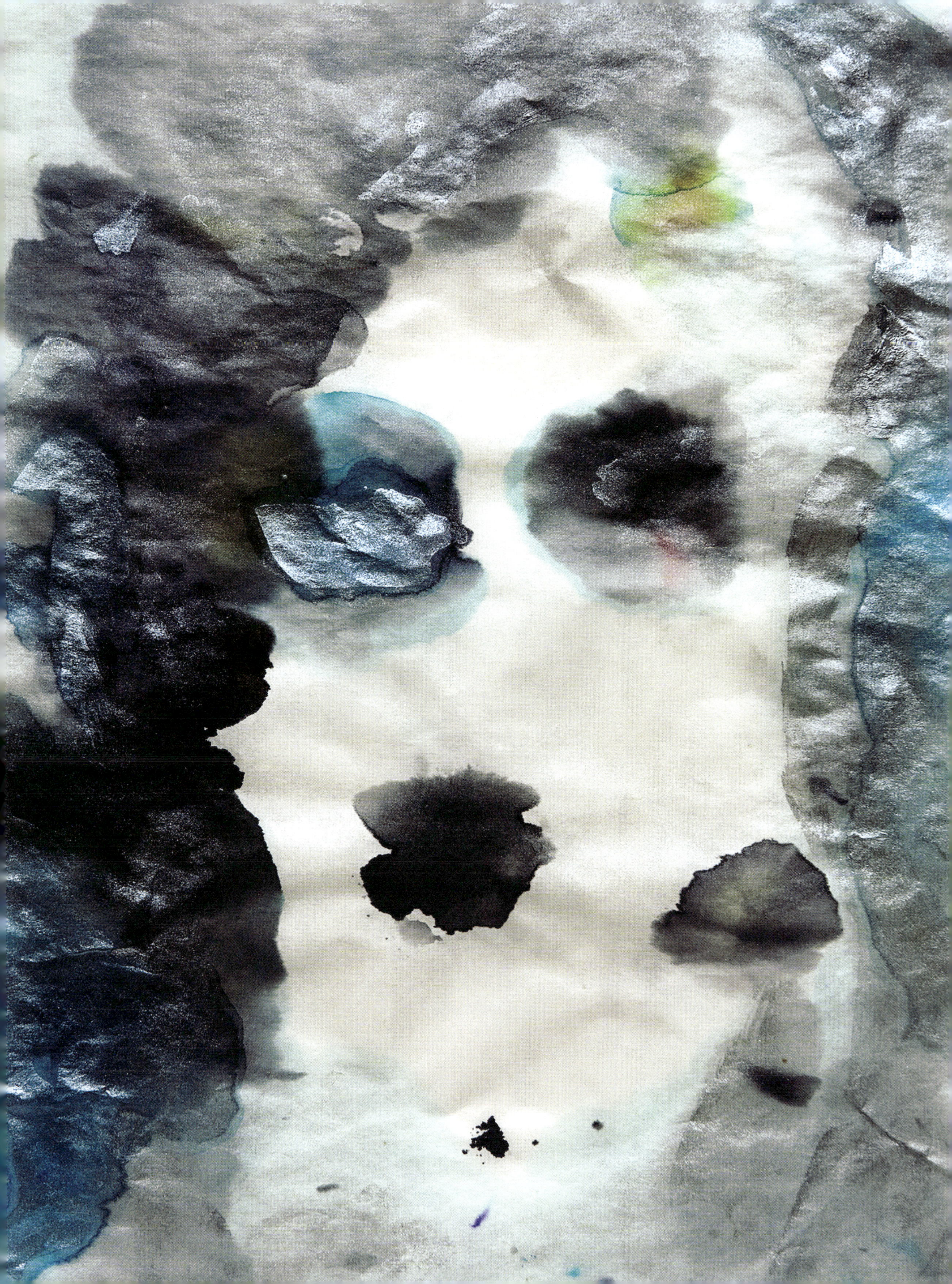

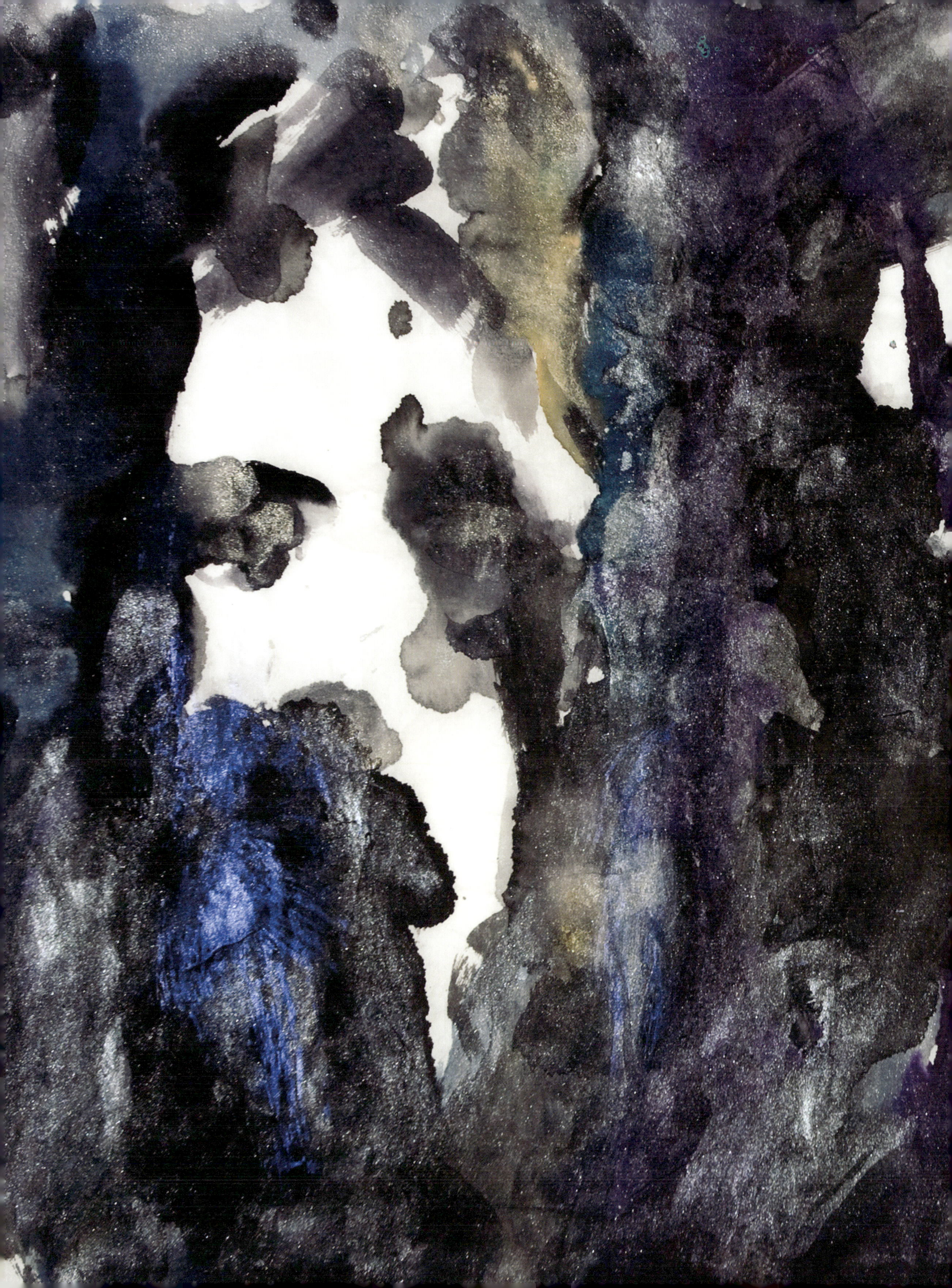

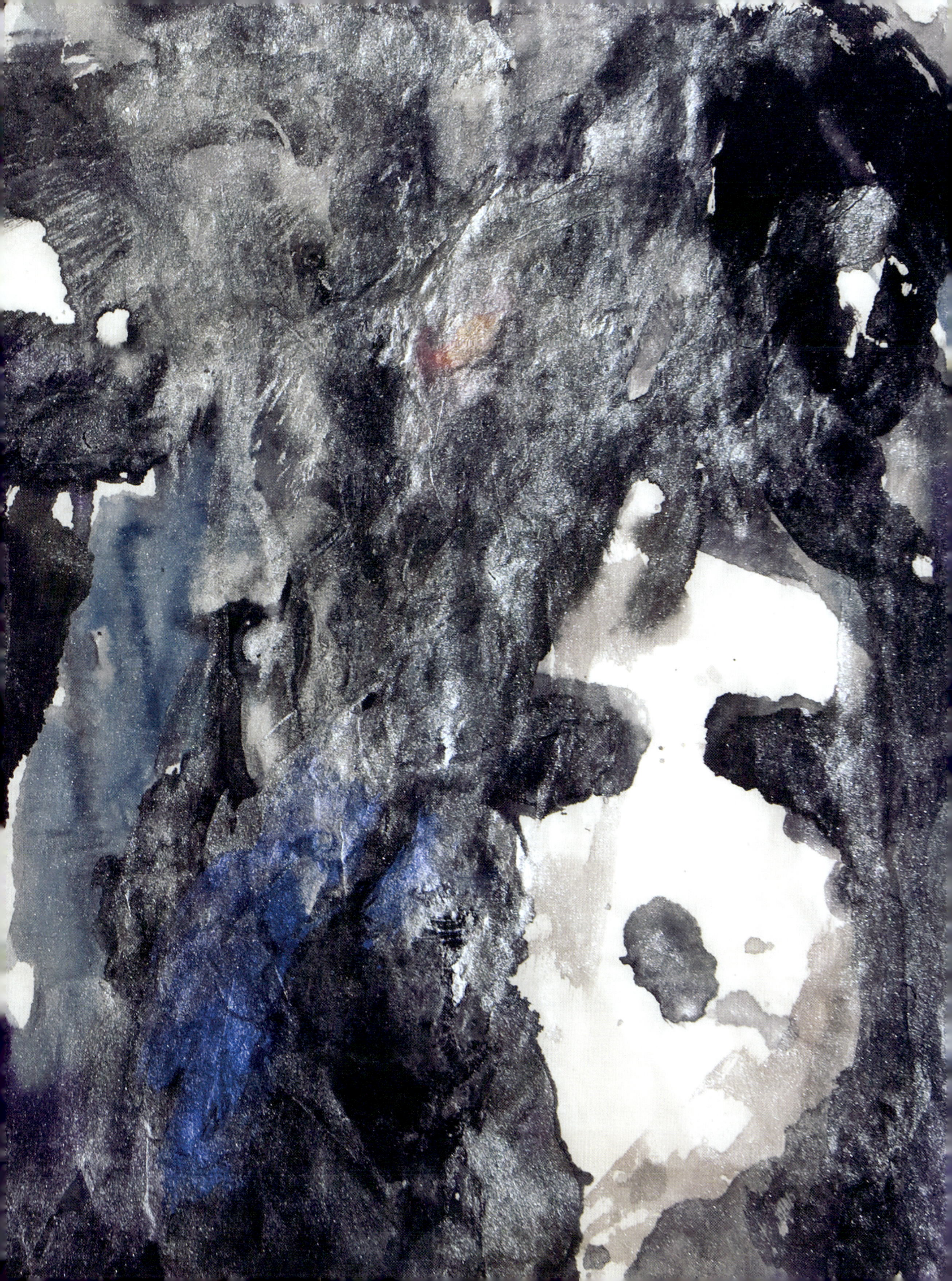

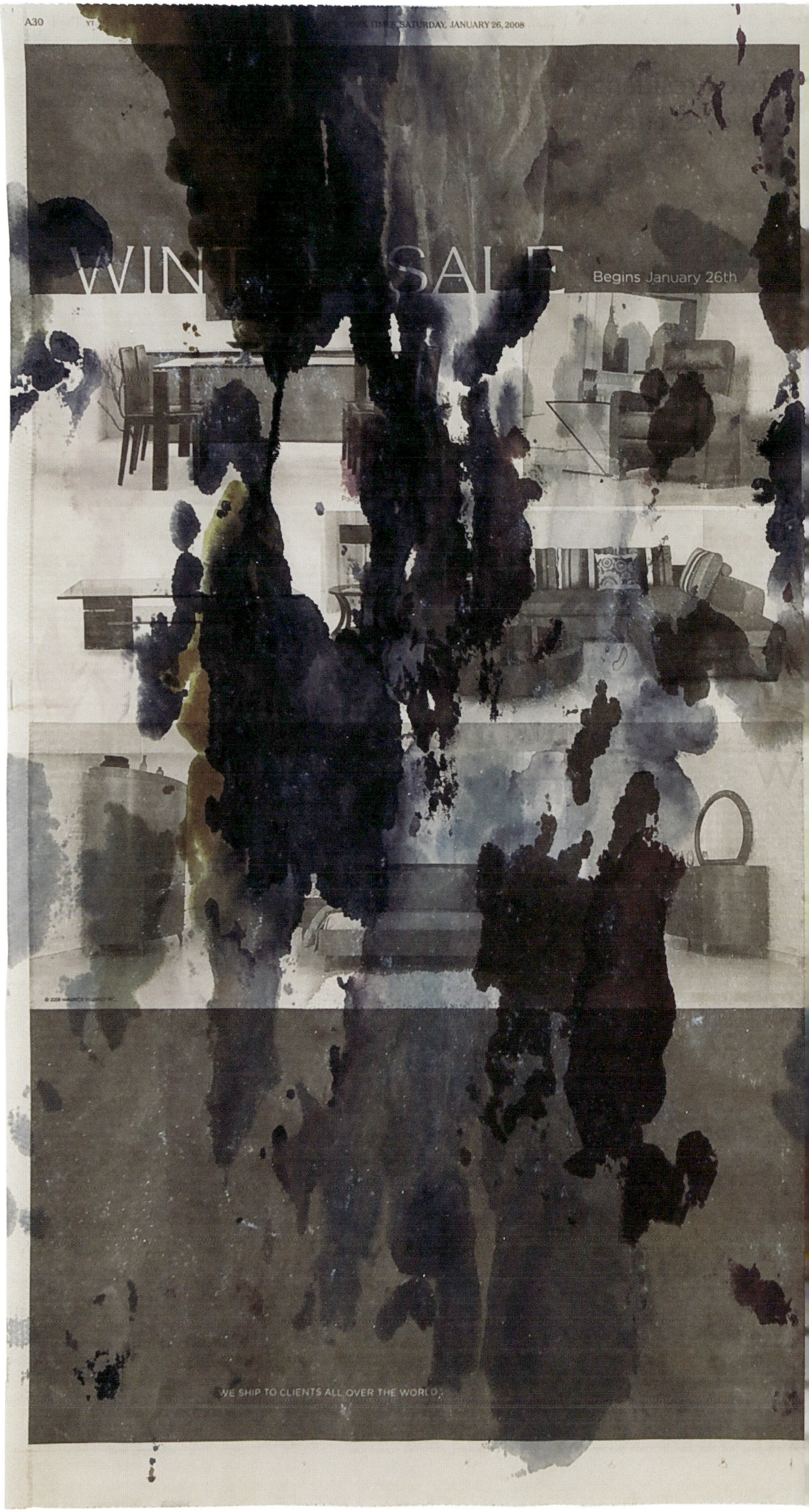
A30
SATURDAY, JANUARY 26, 2008
SALE
Begins January 26th
WE SHIP TO CLIENTS ALL OVER THE WORLD

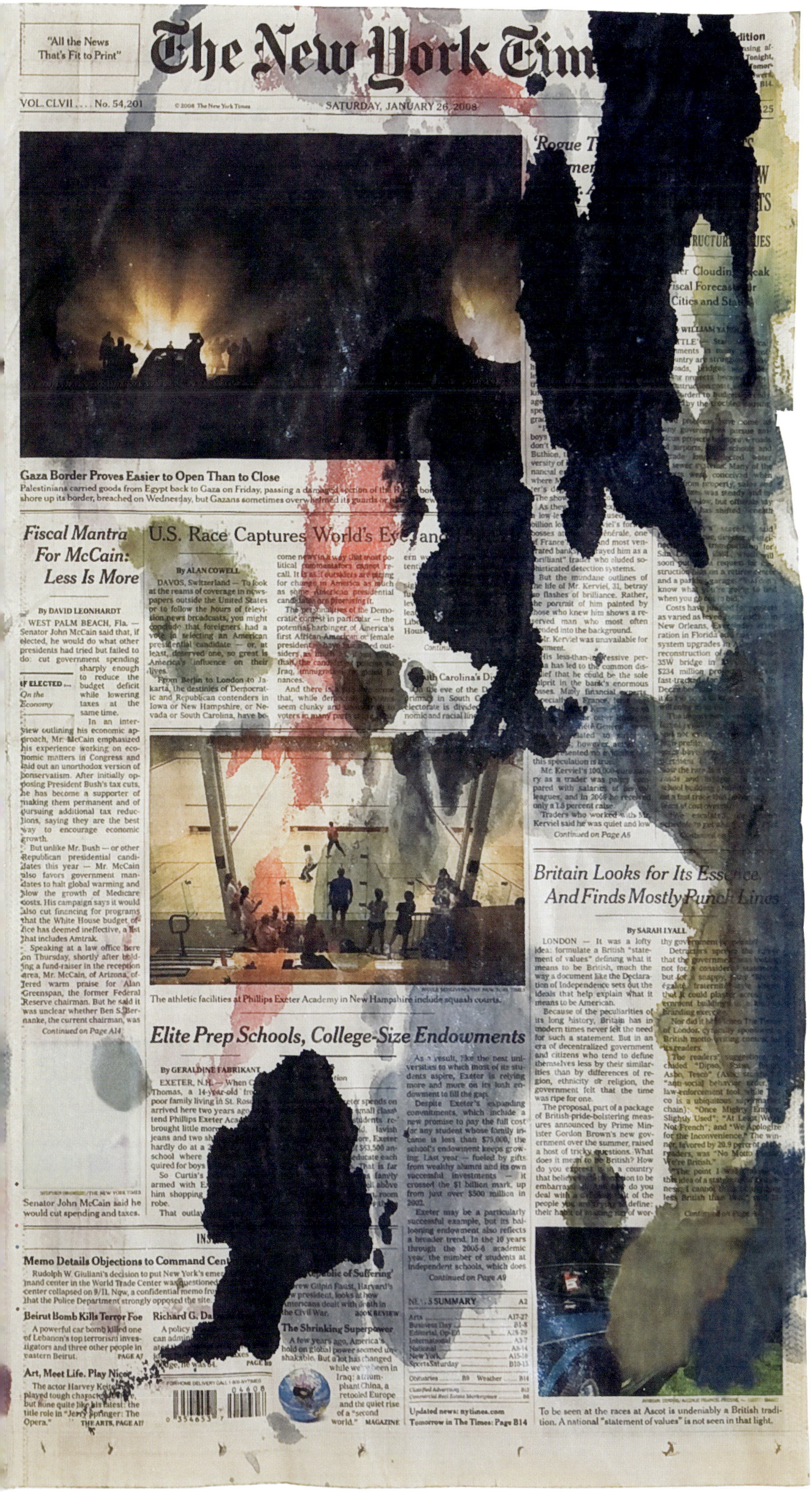
"All the News That's Fit to Print"
The New York Times
VOL. CLVII . . . No. 54,201
SATURDAY, JANUARY 26, 2008
Gaza Border Proves Easier to Open Than to Close
Fiscal Mantra For McCain: Less Is More
By DAVID LEONHARDT
U.S. Race Captures World's Eye
By ALAN COWELL
Britain Looks for Its Essence, And Finds Mostly Punch Lines
By SARAH LYALL
The athletic facilities at Phillips Exeter Academy in New Hampshire include squash courts.
Elite Prep Schools, College-Size Endowments
By GERALDINE FABRIKANT
Senator John McCain said he would cut spending and taxes.
Memo Details Objections to Command Cent
Beirut Bomb Kills Terror Foe
Art, Meet Life. Play Nice
The Shrinking Superpower
NEWS SUMMARY
Updated news: nytimes.com
Tomorrow in The Times: Page B14
To be seen at the races at Ascot is undeniably a British tradition. A national "statement of values" is not seen in that light.

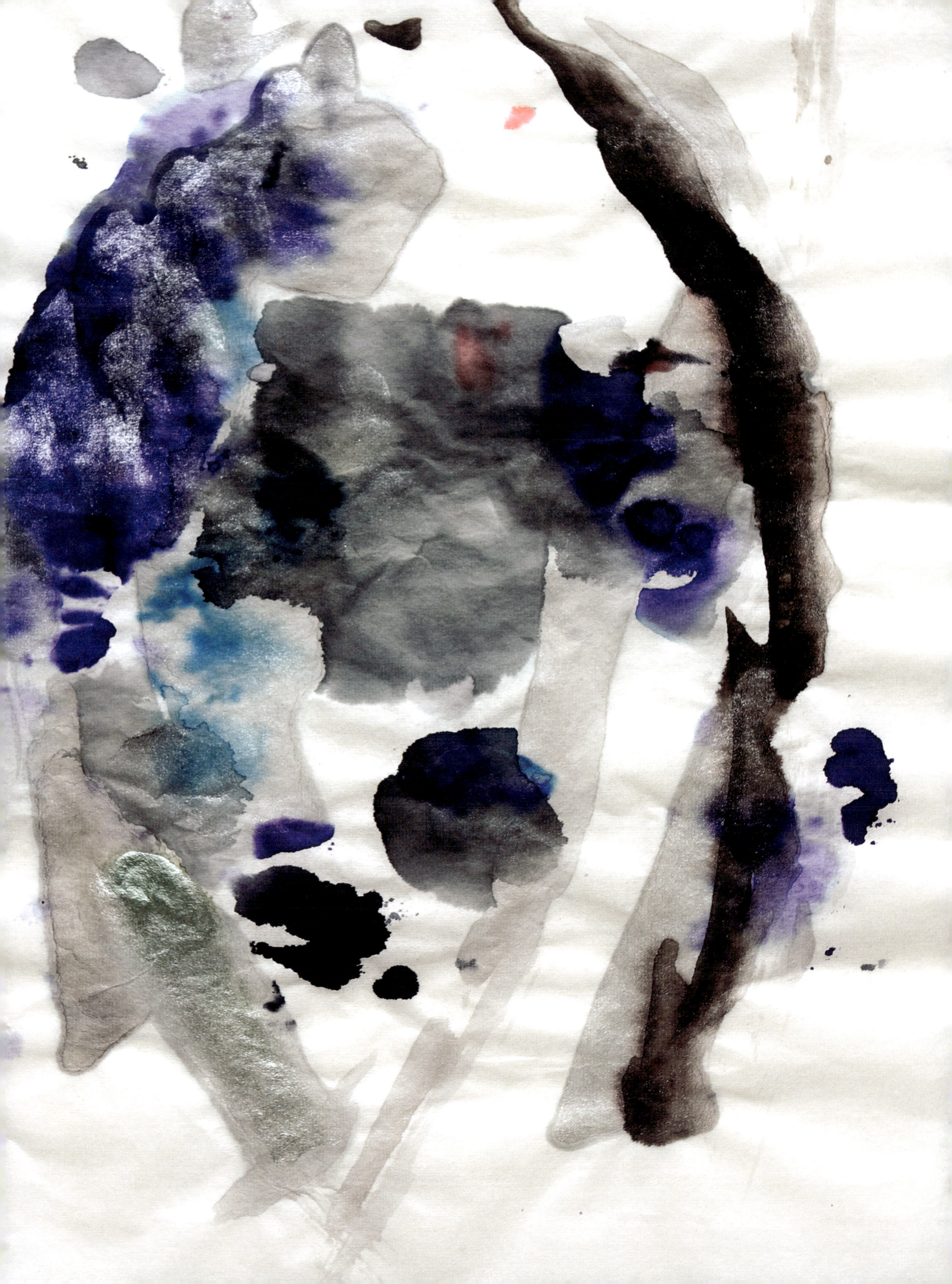

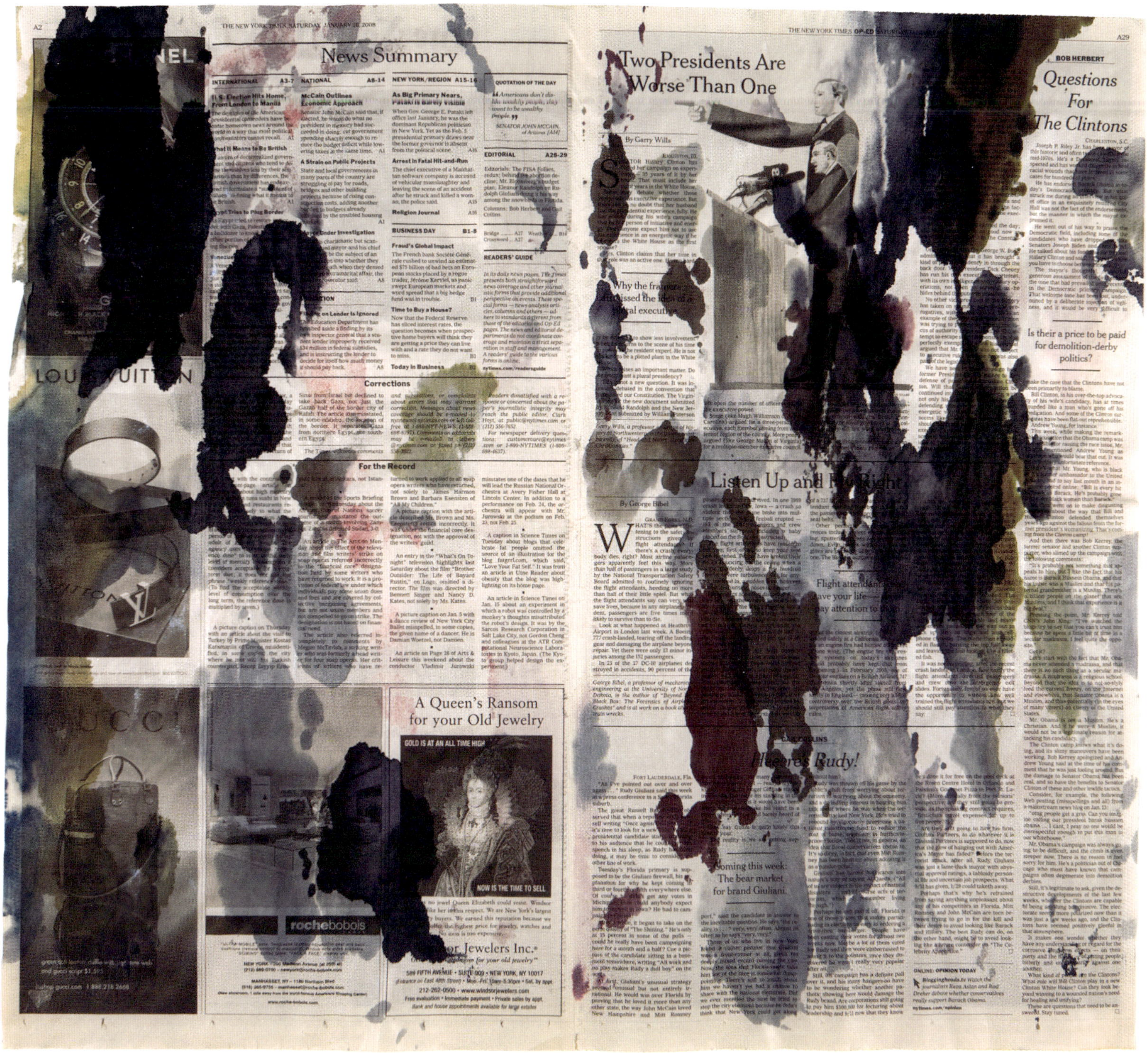
News Summary
Corrections
For the Record
A Queen's Ransom for your Old Jewelry
GOLD IS AT AN ALL TIME HIGH
NOW IS THE TIME TO SELL
589 FIFTH AVENUE • SUITE 909 • NEW YORK, NY 10017
212-262-0500 • www.windsorjewelers.com
LOUIS VUITTON
GUCCI
roche bobois
Two Presidents Are Worse Than One
By Garry Wills
Listen Up and Fly Right
By George Bibel
Questions For The Clintons
BOB HERBERT
Is their a price to be paid for demolition-derby politics?

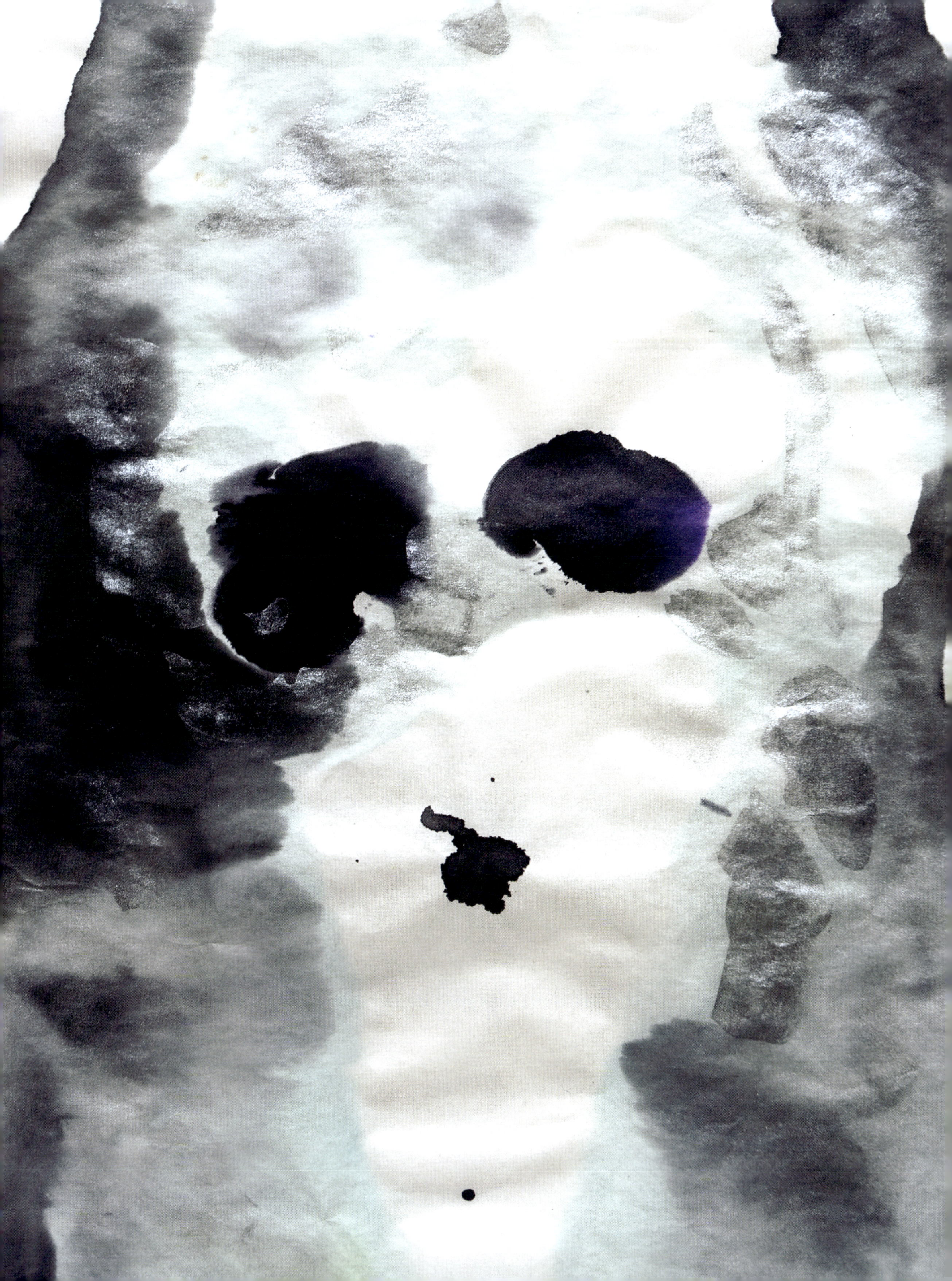

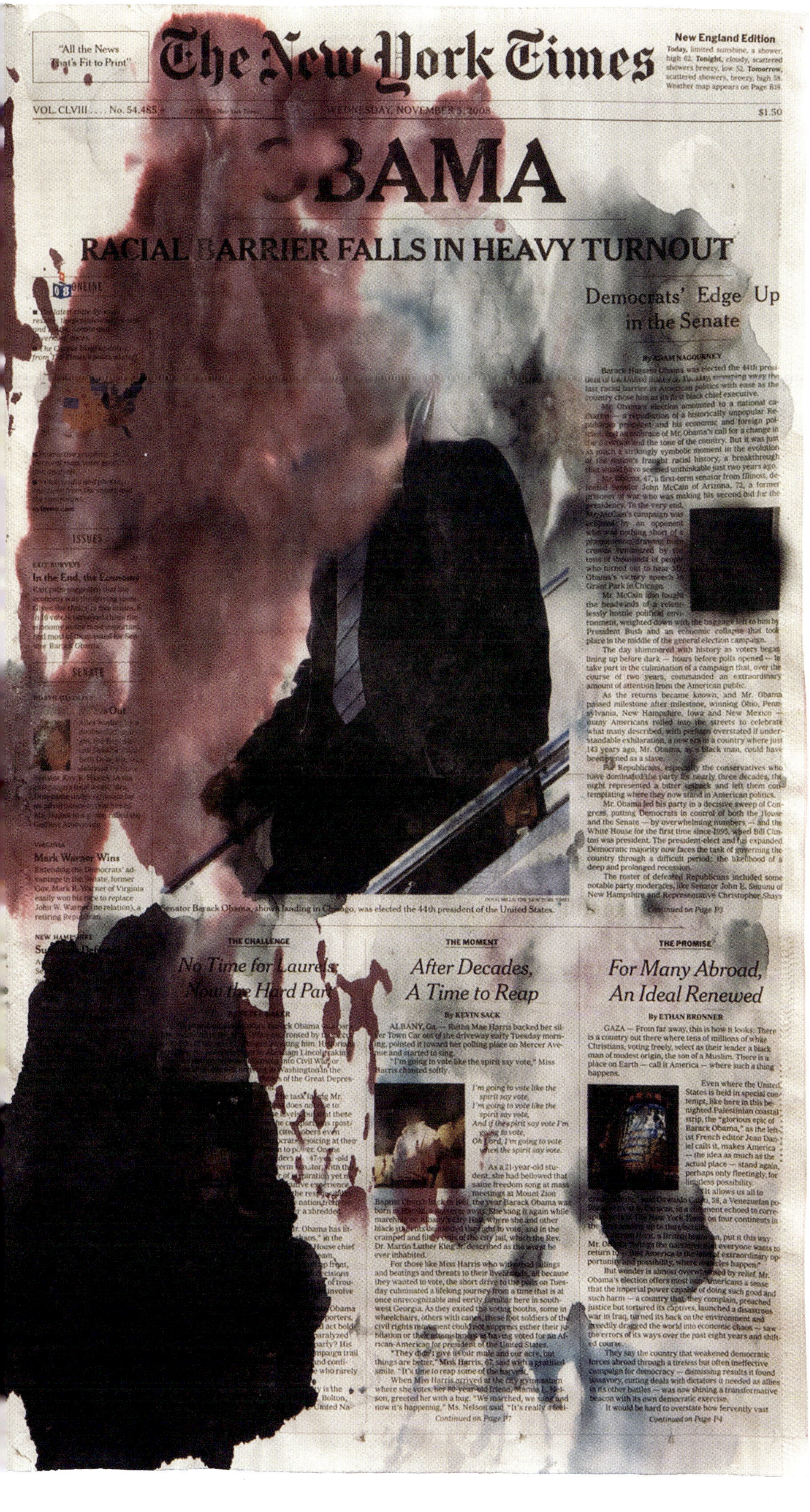

"All the News That's Fit to Print"

The New York Times

New England Edition
Today, limited sunshine, a shower, high 62. **Tonight,** cloudy, scattered showers breezy, low 52. **Tomorrow,** scattered showers, breezy, high 58. Weather map appears on Page B19.

VOL. CLVIII . . . . No. 54,485 — WEDNESDAY, NOVEMBER 5, 2008 — $1.50

OBAMA

RACIAL BARRIER FALLS IN HEAVY TURNOUT

ONLINE

ISSUES

EXIT SURVEYS

In the End, the Economy

SENATE

VIRGINIA

Mark Warner Wins

Extending the Democrats' advantage in the Senate, former Gov. Mark R. Warner of Virginia easily won his race to replace John W. Warner (no relation), a retiring Republican.

NEW HAMPSHIRE

Democrats' Edge Up in the Senate

By ADAM NAGOURNEY

Barack Hussein Obama was elected the 44th president of the United States on Tuesday, sweeping away the last racial barrier in American politics with ease as the country chose him as its first black chief executive.

Mr. Obama's election amounted to a national catharsis — a repudiation of a historically unpopular Republican president and his economic and foreign policies, and an embrace of Mr. Obama's call for a change in the direction and the tone of the country. But it was just as much a strikingly symbolic moment in the evolution of the nation's fraught racial history, a breakthrough that would have seemed unthinkable just two years ago.

Mr. Obama, 47, a first-term senator from Illinois, defeated Senator John McCain of Arizona, 72, a former prisoner of war who was making his second bid for the presidency. To the very end, Mr. McCain's campaign was eclipsed by an opponent who was nothing short of a phenomenon, drawing huge crowds epitomized by the tens of thousands of people who turned out to hear Mr. Obama's victory speech in Grant Park in Chicago.

Mr. McCain also fought the headwinds of a relentlessly hostile political environment, weighted down with the baggage left to him by President Bush and an economic collapse that took place in the middle of the general election campaign.

The day shimmered with history as voters began lining up before dark — hours before polls opened — to take part in the culmination of a campaign that, over the course of two years, commanded an extraordinary amount of attention from the American public.

As the returns became known, and Mr. Obama passed milestone after milestone, winning Ohio, Pennsylvania, New Hampshire, Iowa and New Mexico — many Americans rolled into the streets to celebrate what many described, with perhaps overstated if understandable exhilaration, a new era in a country where just 143 years ago, Mr. Obama, as a black man, could have been owned as a slave.

For Republicans, especially the conservatives who have dominated the party for nearly three decades, the night represented a bitter setback and left them contemplating where they now stand in American politics.

Mr. Obama led his party in a decisive sweep of Congress, putting Democrats in control of both the House and the Senate — by overwhelming numbers — and the White House for the first time since 1995, when Bill Clinton was president. The president-elect and his expanded Democratic majority now faces the task of governing the country through a difficult period: the likelihood of a deep and prolonged recession.

The roster of defeated Republicans included some notable party moderates, like Senator John E. Sununu of New Hampshire and Representative Christopher Shays

Continued on Page P3

DOUG MILLS/THE NEW YORK TIMES

Senator Barack Obama, shown landing in Chicago, was elected the 44th president of the United States.

THE CHALLENGE

No Time for Laurels; Now the Hard Part

THE MOMENT

After Decades, A Time to Reap

By KEVIN SACK

ALBANY, Ga. — Rutha Mae Harris backed her silver Town Car out of the driveway early Tuesday morning, pointed it toward her polling place on Mercer Avenue and started to sing.

"I'm going to vote like the spirit say vote," Miss Harris chanted softly.

I'm going to vote like the spirit say vote,
I'm going to vote like the spirit say vote,
And if the spirit say vote I'm going to vote,
Oh Lord, I'm going to vote when the spirit say vote.

As a 21-year-old student, she had bellowed that same freedom song at mass meetings at Mount Zion Baptist Church back in 1961, the year Barack Obama was born in Hawaii, a universe away. She sang it again while marching on Albany's City Hall, where she and other black students demanded the right to vote, and in the cramped and filthy cells of the city jail, which the Rev. Dr. Martin Luther King Jr. described as the worst he ever inhabited.

For those like Miss Harris who withstood jailings and beatings and threats to their livelihoods, all because they wanted to vote, the short drive to the polls on Tuesday culminated a lifelong journey from a time that is at once unrecognizable and eerily familiar here in southwest Georgia. As they exited the voting booths, some in wheelchairs, others with canes, these foot soldiers of the civil rights movement could not suppress either their jubilation or their astonishment at having voted for an African-American for president of the United States.

"They didn't give us our mule and our acre, but things are better," Miss Harris, 67, said with a gratified smile. "It's time to reap some of the harvest."

When Miss Harris arrived at the city gymnasium where she votes, her 60-year-old friend, Mamie L. Nelson, greeted her with a hug. "We marched, we sang and now it's happening," Ms. Nelson said. "It's really a feel-

Continued on Page P7

THE PROMISE

For Many Abroad, An Ideal Renewed

By ETHAN BRONNER

GAZA — From far away, this is how it looks: There is a country out there where tens of millions of white Christians, voting freely, select as their leader a black man of modest origin, the son of a Muslim. There is a place on Earth — call it America — where such a thing happens.

Even where the United States is held in special contempt, like here in this benighted Palestinian coastal strip, the "glorious epic of Barack Obama," as the leftist French editor Jean Daniel calls it, makes America — the idea as much as the actual place — stand again, perhaps only fleetingly, for limitless possibility.

"It allows us all to [illegible]," said Oswaldo Ca[illegible], 58, a Venezuelan po[illegible] in Caracas, in a comment echoed to correspondents of The New York Times on four continents in the days leading up to the election.

[illegible], a British historian, put it this way: Mr. Obama "brings the narrative that everyone wants to return to — that America is the land of extraordinary opportunity and possibility, where miracles happen."

But wonder is almost overwhelmed by relief. Mr. Obama's election offers most non-Americans a sense that the imperial power capable of doing such good and such harm — a country that, they complain, preached justice but tortured its captives, launched a disastrous war in Iraq, turned its back on the environment and greedily dragged the world into economic chaos — saw the errors of its ways over the past eight years and shifted course.

They say the country that weakened democratic forces abroad through a tireless but often ineffective campaign for democracy — dismissing results it found unsavory, cutting deals with dictators it needed as allies in its other battles — was now shining a transformative beacon with its own democratic exercise.

It would be hard to overstate how fervently vast

Continued on Page P4

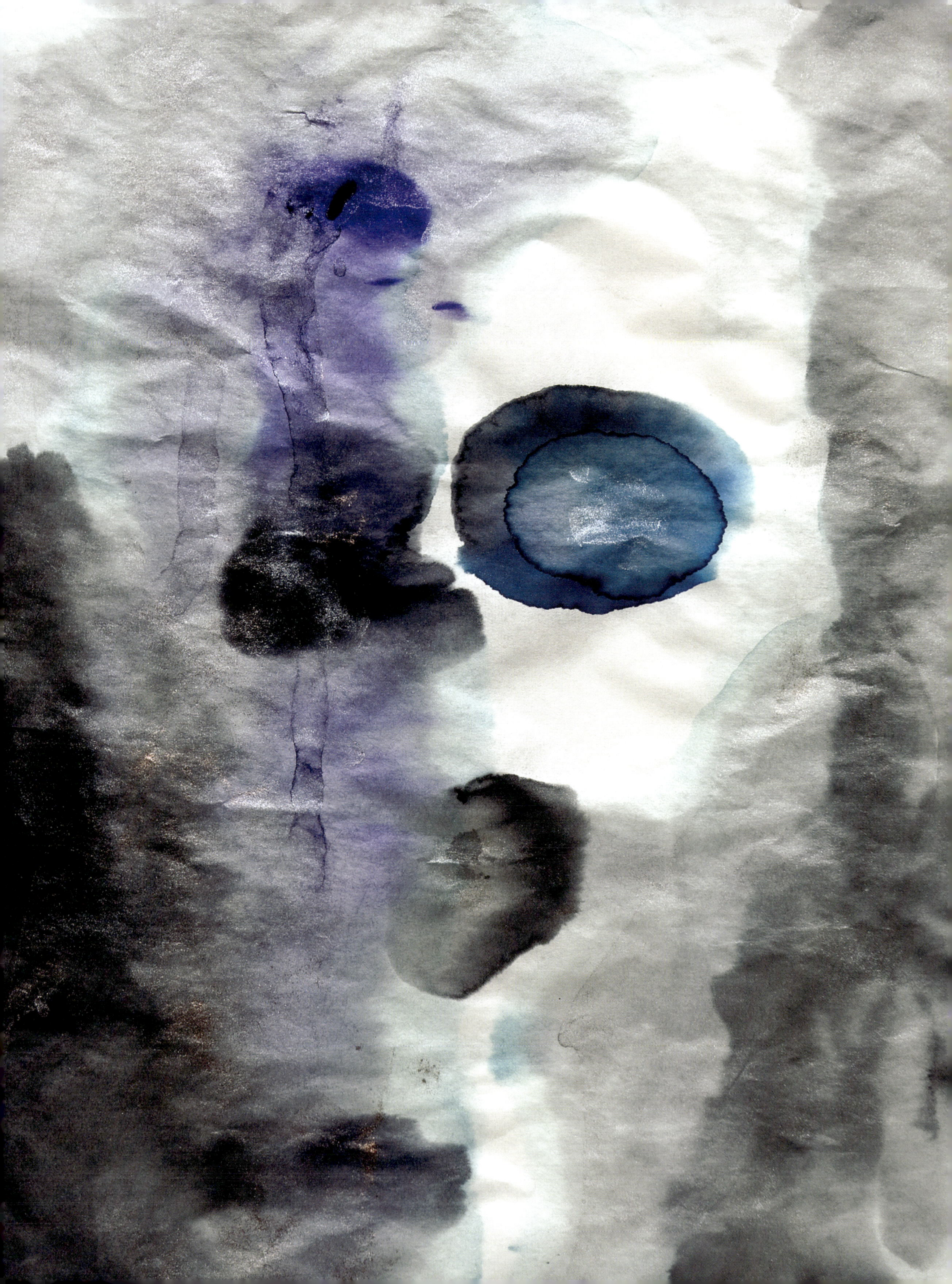

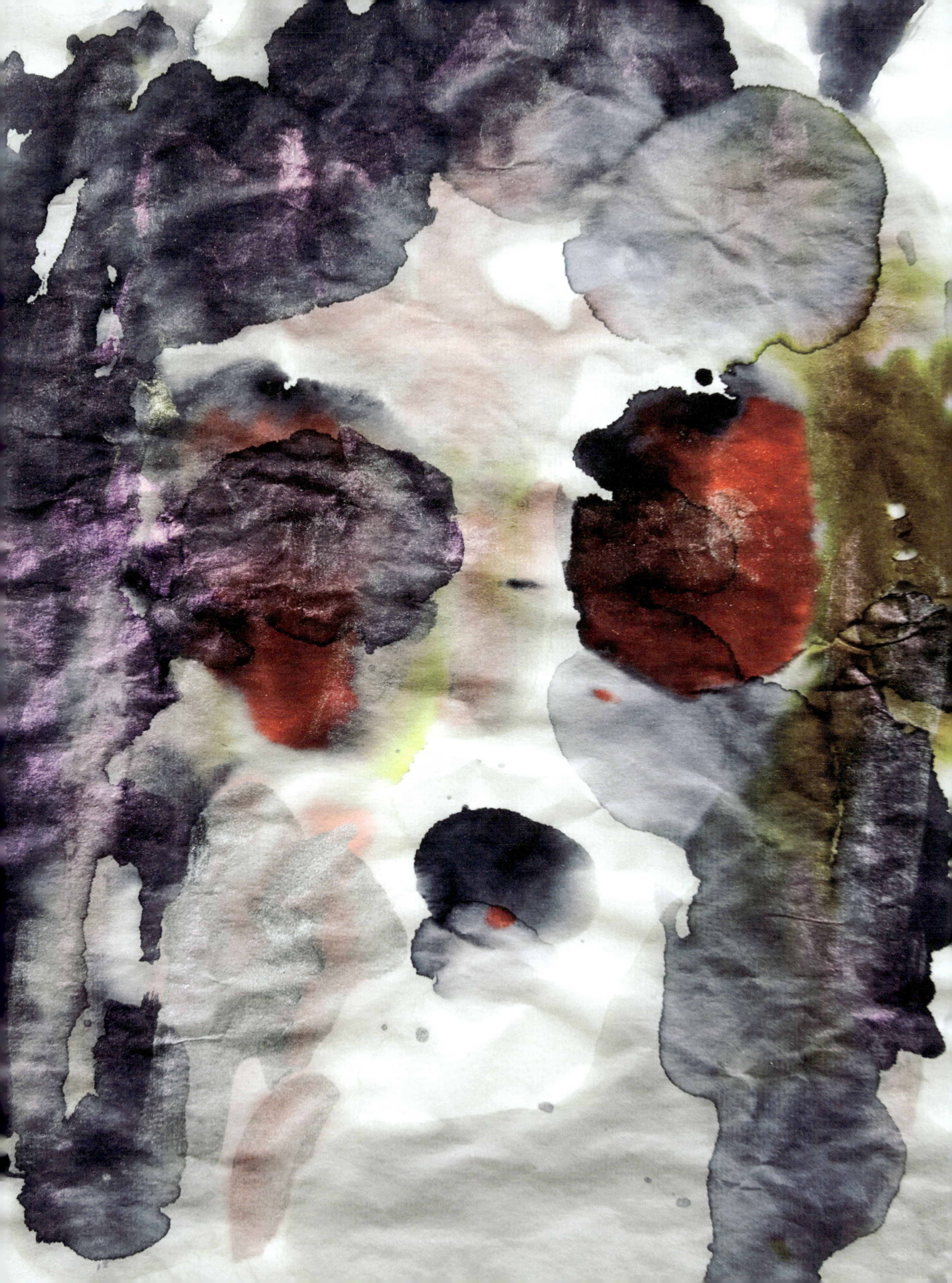

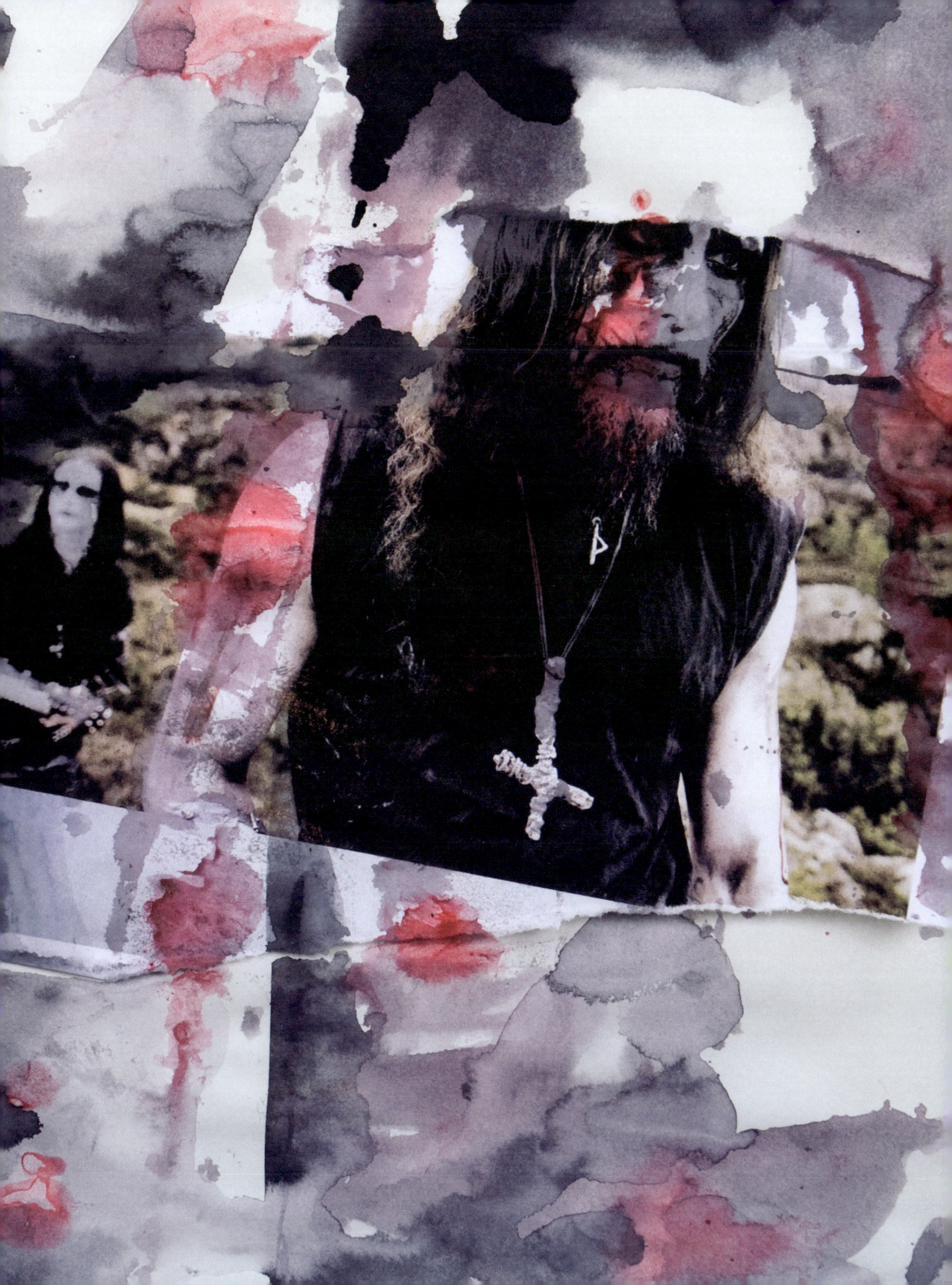

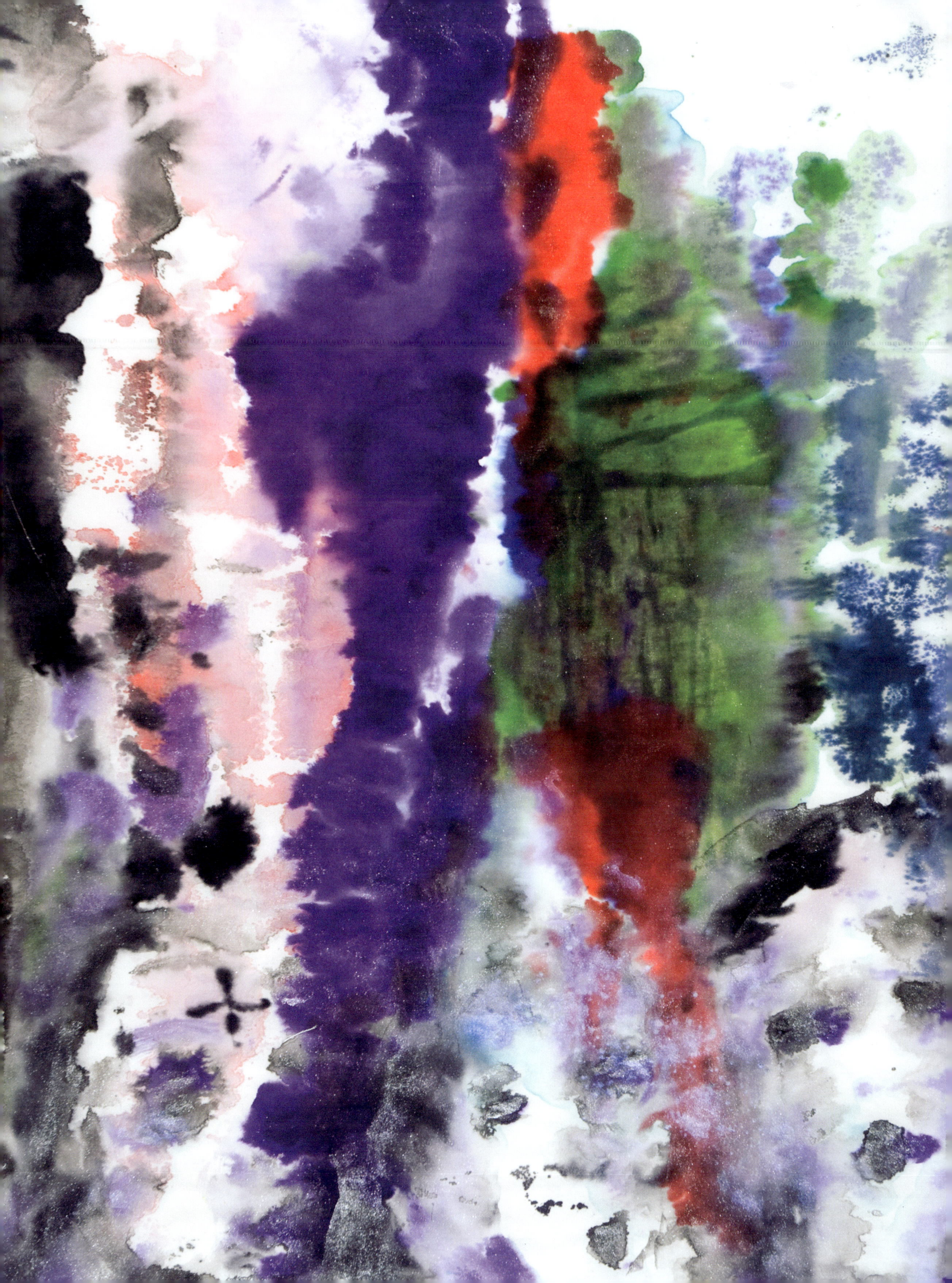

Standing in the hall watching the band I could barely breathe. The top half of my back felt really heavy making it difficult to stand up straight. I shifted my weight from the left hip to the right hip. Every so often I felt relief in a large deep breath in and out. My left shoulder ached from the weight of my purse. I circled around to the other side of the crowd, weaving in and out of people, sometimes walking sideways thru people. I shifted my weight again back and forth. The music was incredibly loud. It was boring so I moved to the back and then left.

He swayed back and looked out at the audience unsure as to whether he should venture to the front of the stage. The sound behind him started out quiet, almost tentatively. The two guitars met in the middle and wove their way thru the room hitting him in the back and circling around either side. He splayed his body out on the rug and turned up the volume. The voice was almost inaudible. What were they expecting. He took a hit off the joint and leaned back, he only felt at home on stage. He had to get stoned in order to enjoy his living room.

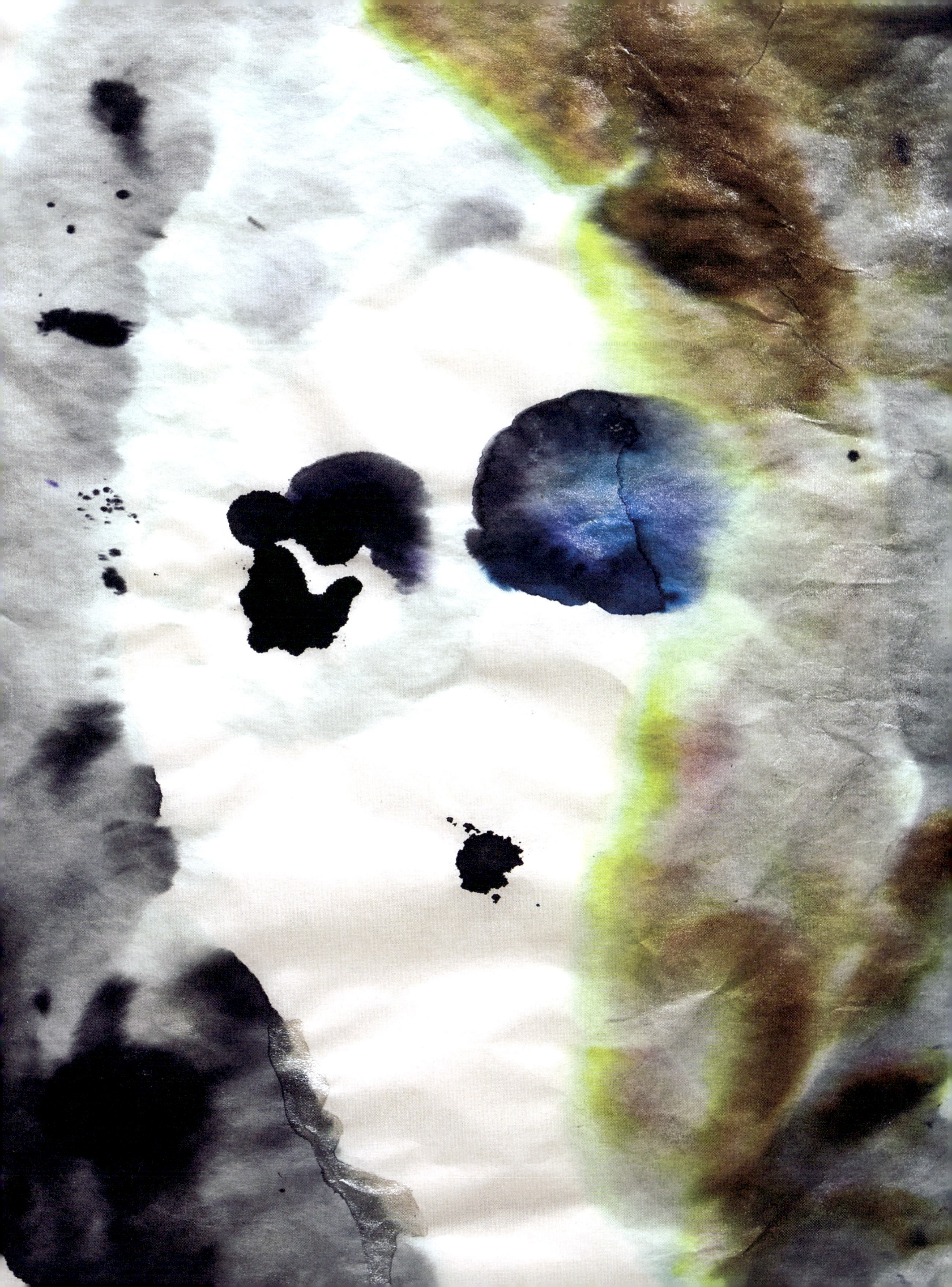

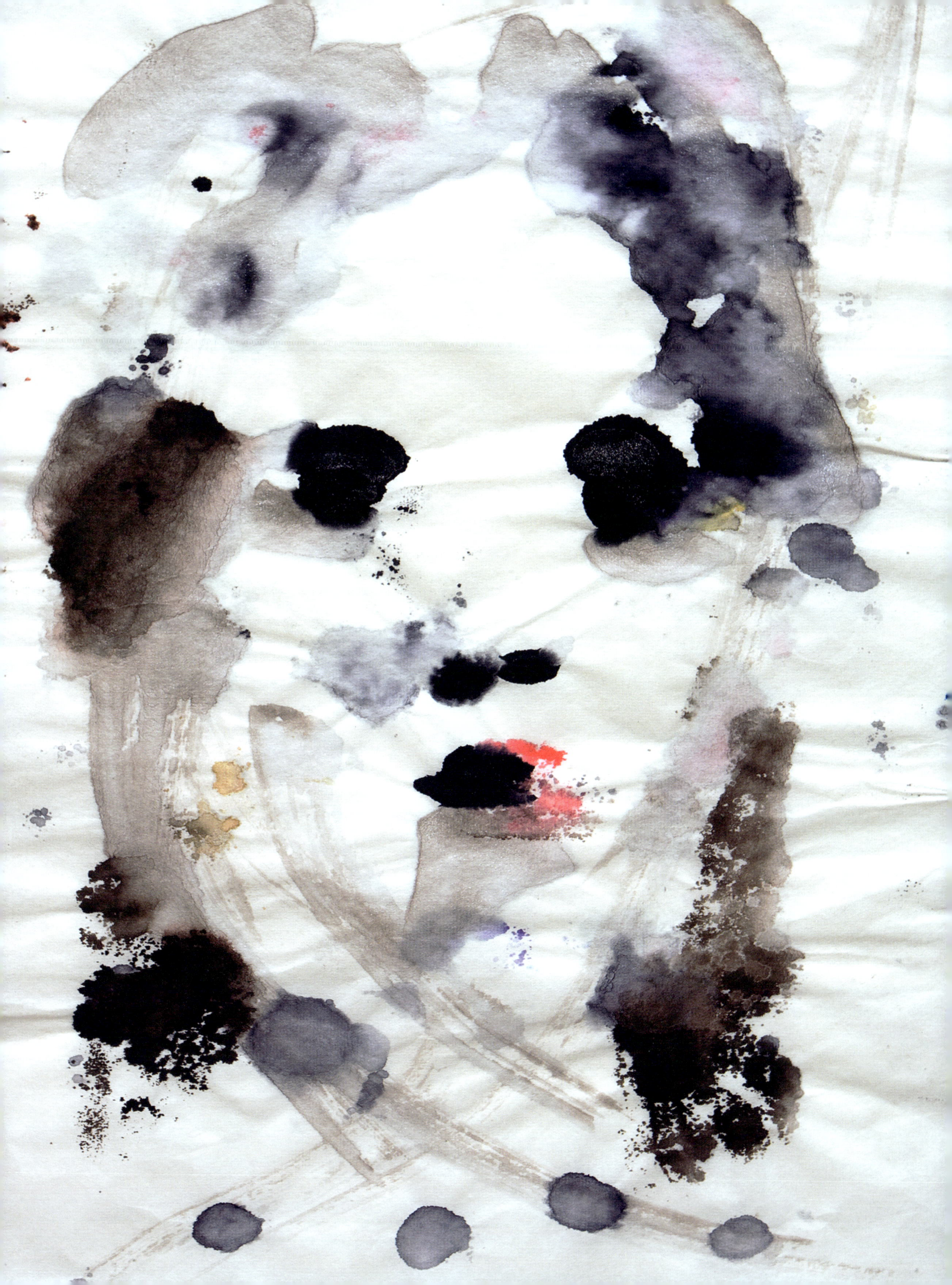

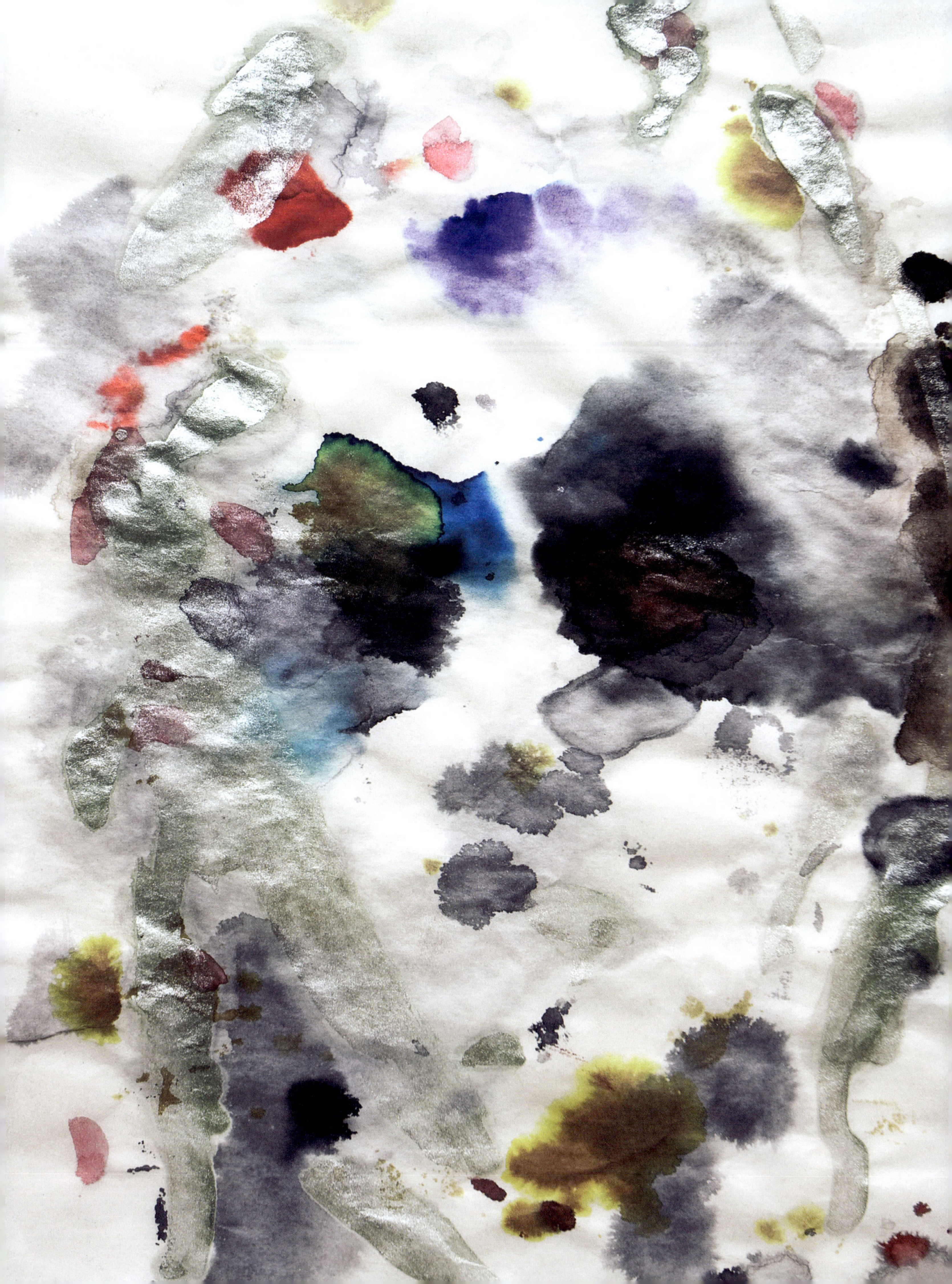

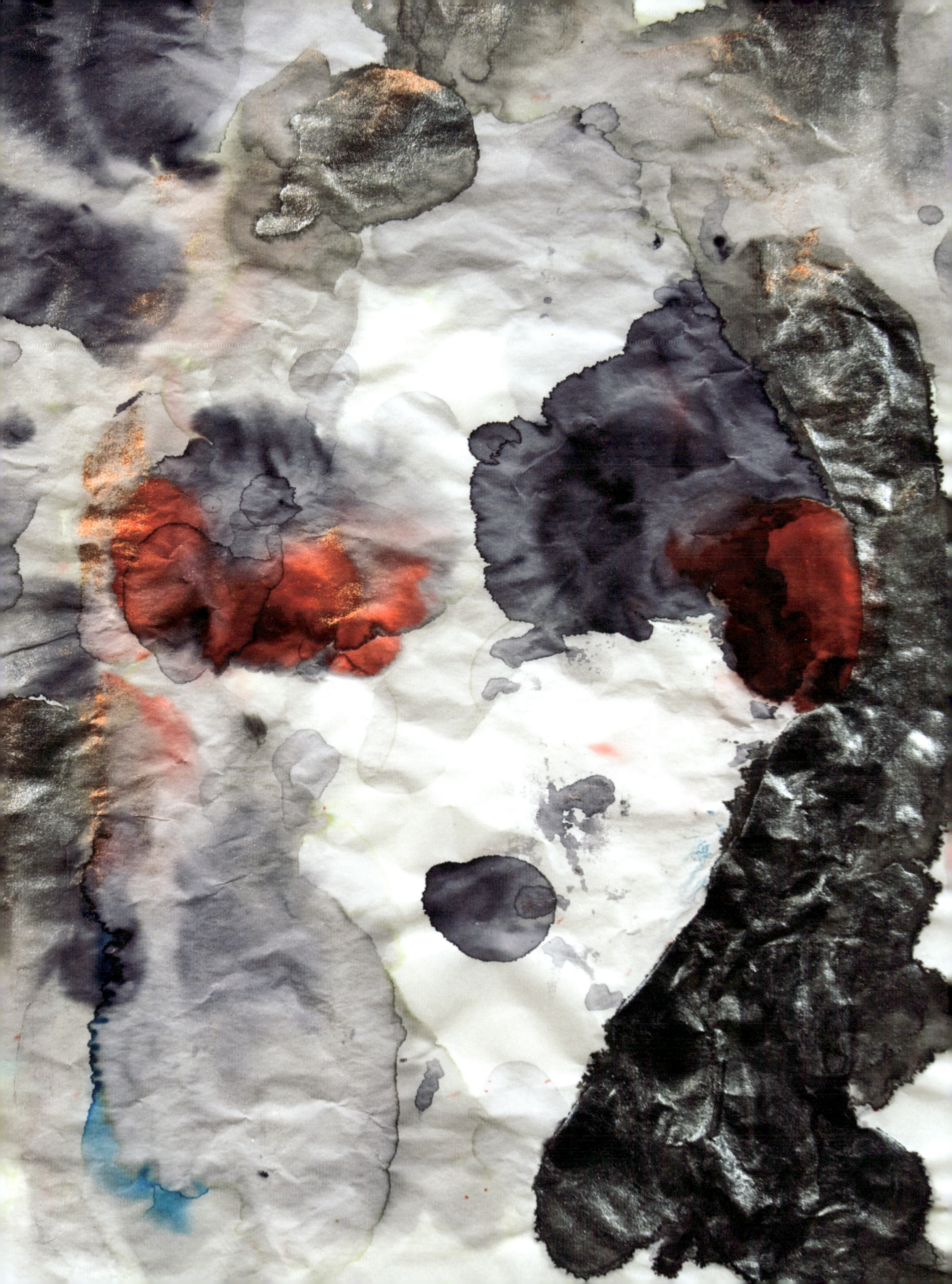

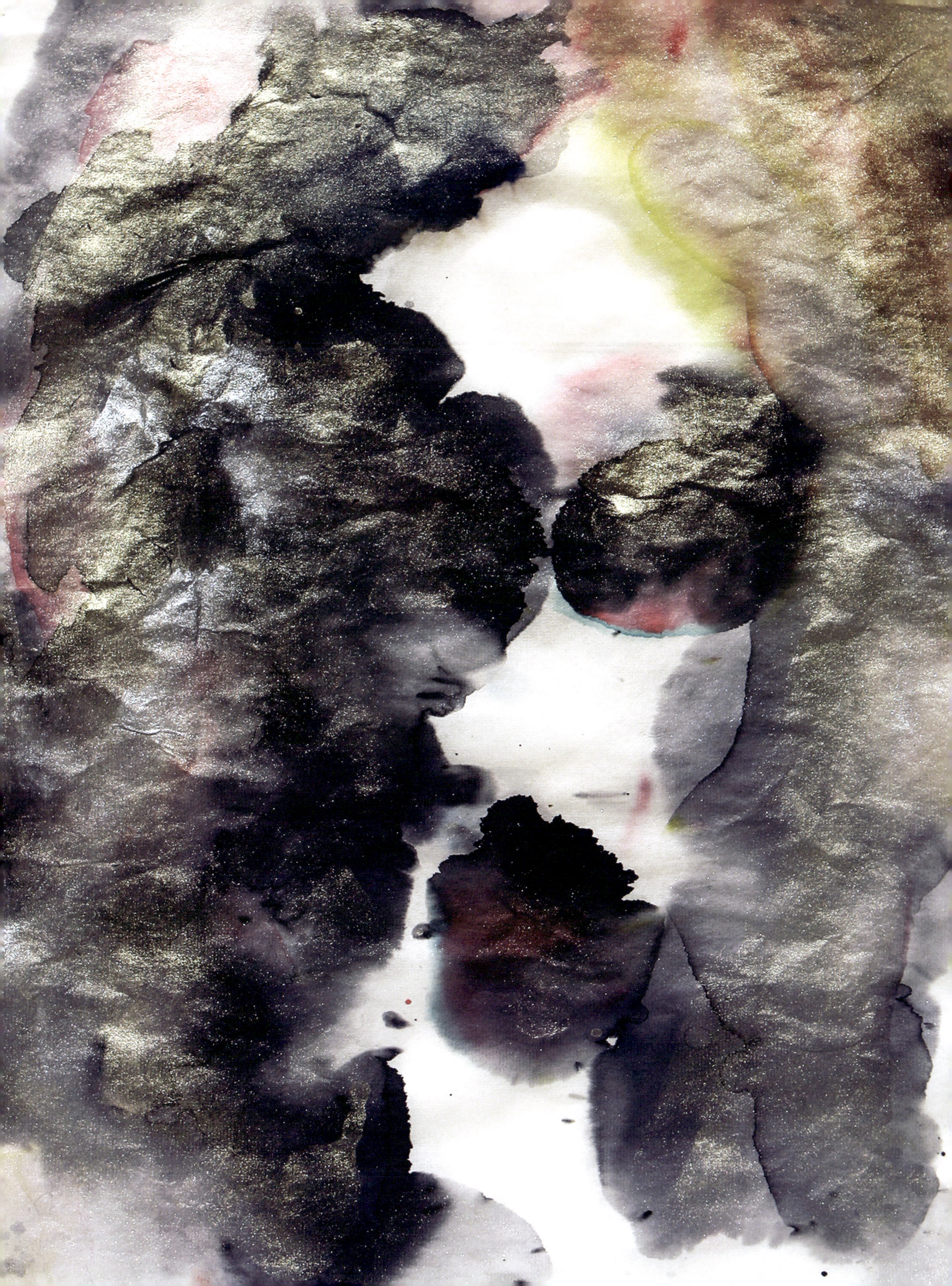

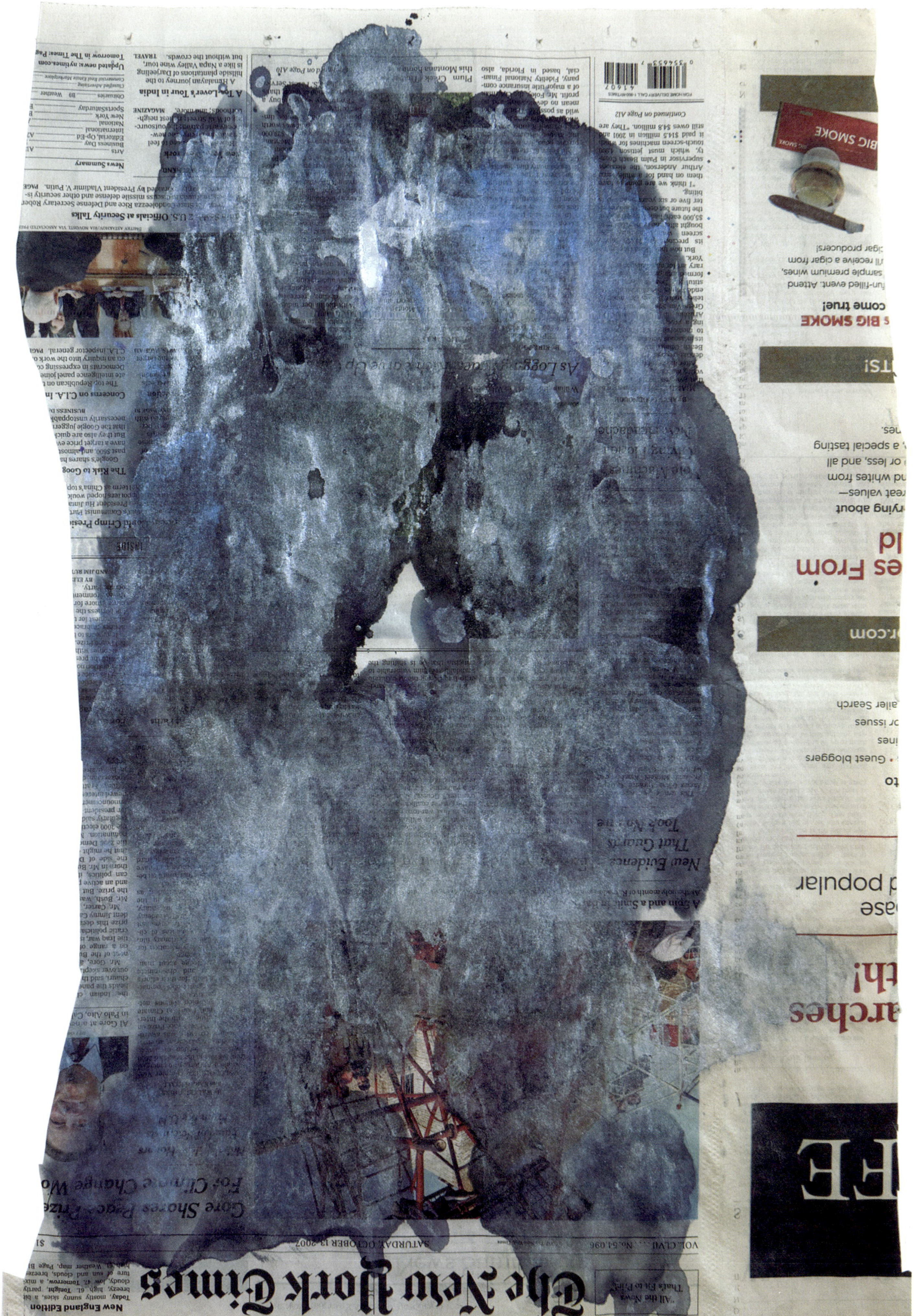

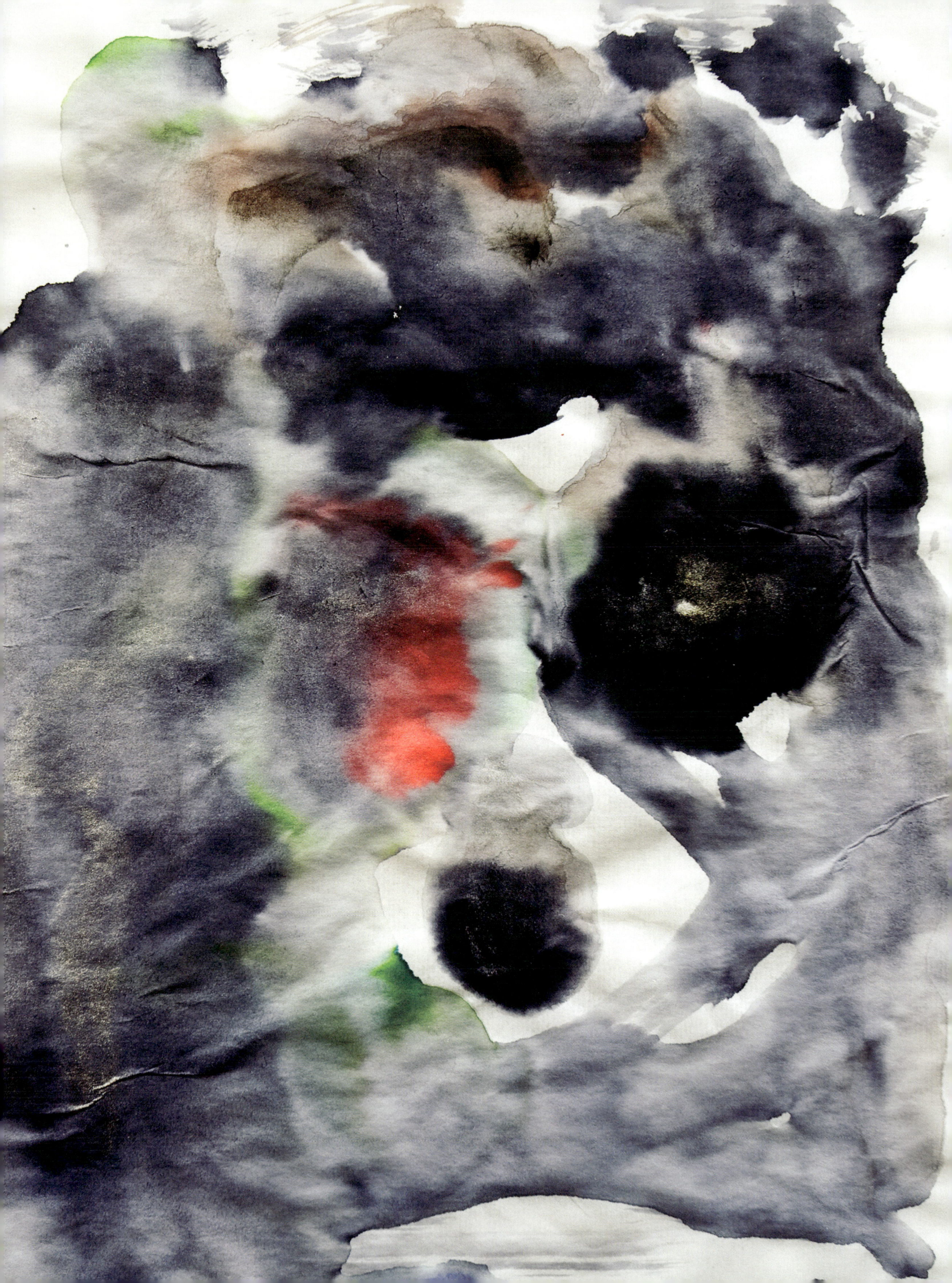

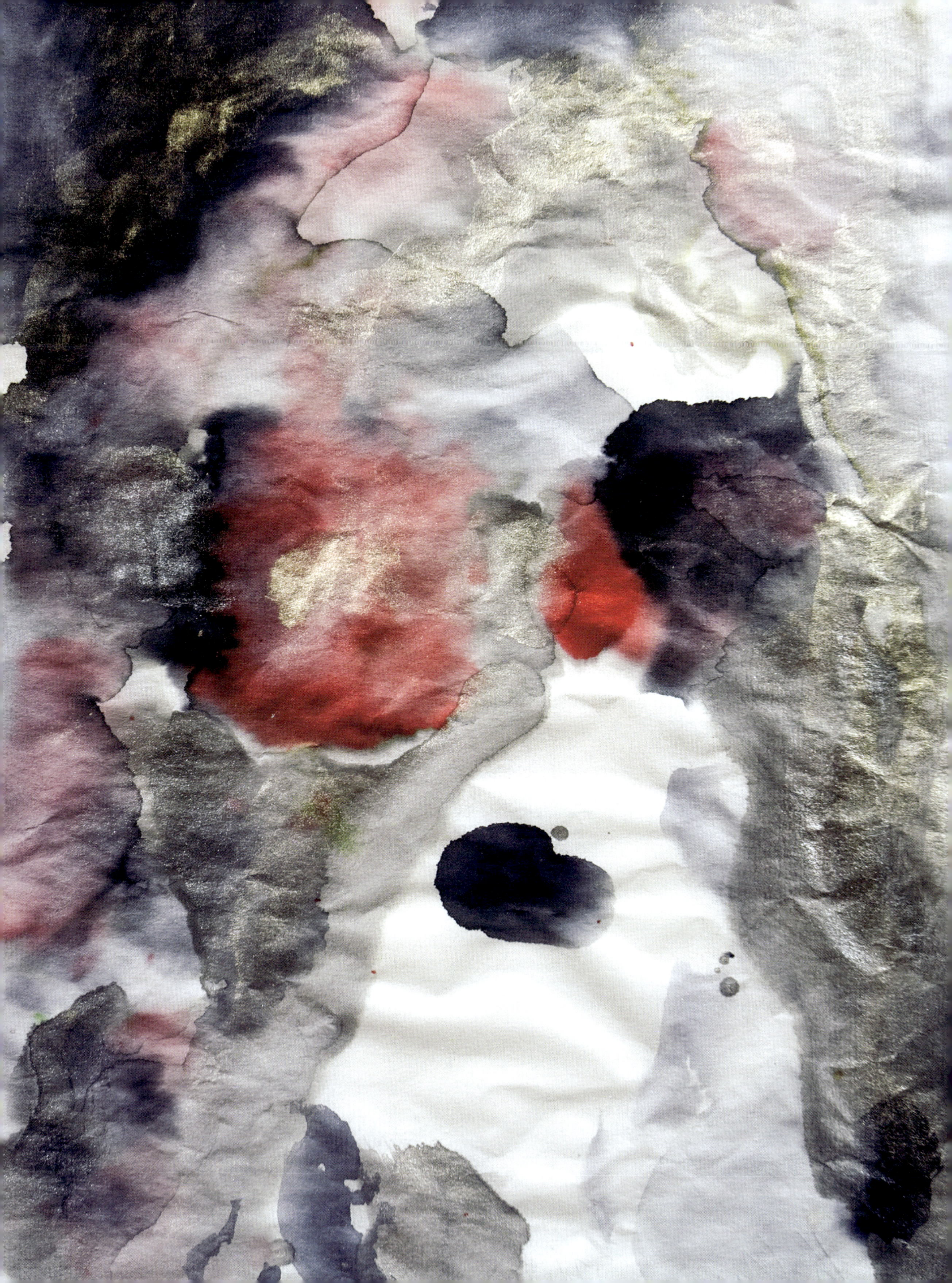

Harsh Pastoral

"…to expose oneself to one's own un-groundedness…"
†

Fearlessly doing so. Seeing, drowning, shivering.

Here are a few words regarding Kim's watercolor face works, thoughts mounted in the styles of Kim´s watercolor faces:

Sentences from a blotched, harsh pastoral that form a face, somehow, which starts saying sth… Dissolves. Re-forms from itself—whatever it is.

I have followed these particular works of Kim's because they continue to cross my path. They are full-on, direct, almost unmediated. Yet they are templates. Stand-ins. Detached. I consider them the most personal, and at the same time the most universal, part of her artistic work.

They keep crossing my own painting path and hold my interest in painting-as-woman. Kim's paintings stare out of dead eyes. (Check out Cézanne's early painting *The Eternal Female*.) Allegorical women—but some who do not represent anything. Rules of beauty, responsibility, symbolic content—all suspended. All washed away.

They form formless conjunctions, puddles between articulations, displays of passion, gaze and non-gaze. The female idol multiplied, casual, misplaced. Defiance re-articulated over and over again by those non-eyes.

Those heads might not all be intended as female heads. But they lend themselves to support my interests, and I hope they don't mind.

The Sovereign Woman in Painting as articulated by Jean-Luc Nancy:

"Antiquity created the oxymoron of the sovereign woman in love. Neither sovereignty nor love owes anything to anyone or to anything other than itself, and this unparalleled sufficiency is also their extraordinary fragility. They are, each of them, what they are only insomuch as they renounce their own ground and therefore are capable ultimately, of renouncing themselves."

They maintain a kind of infectious anarchy, being pictures for private aesthetic and intellectual stimulation—needs of the spirit.

"Art becomes the sovereign neither of the world nor of the souls but of the very enigma of sovereignty of the paradox and ambiguity that arise when sovereignty is no longer hierophantic: that is, of the possibility of founding without a foundation, and of making laws without legislation."

In that sense, they lay down the law.

(And this, I might add to place Kim the performer back into the picture, very much relates to the way she swings her guitar or dances around on a stage.)

Bright death pictures.
Even the sweeter faces carry some odd, soft damage. Faces blotched by water into hazy, painterly abstractness.
Harsh pastorals. Somewhere in there is always a Death Valley.
Those darkish spots.
Her darkness. From a ground that is without depth:
Then light, a gaze appearing, not directed by any ideality.

Night effects.

Not necessarily hidden meanings—but there seems to be always sth bubbling up. A reaction. Water meets paint on a piece of paper. Hair dissolves like a note, forms a feedback noise. Or an angry piece of an eye. There is a search for sensual presence, then a drift into nothing. There is an Ophelia effect. Dead already. Stuck in water. A zombie— always beautiful, even in utter ghoulishness. There is the theme of blindness and seeing. There is sound in there: muffled noises, chatter, bubbling up, making an appearance, a going under or just away.

It is all transformed into a moment of art that performs itself, only to let it go again.

A fearless drowning.

It is a somewhat disturbed art—or the face as a disturbing place, becoming a site, rather.

They are painted with the colors of yearning. They are like dirty mirrors—yet the structural and material conditions of the pieces do not sublimate or replace desire but produce it in defiance of the willfully distorted, watery faces on display.

In one of her texts, Kim describes how she experiences the audience forming a collective mood and how that experience stimulates and informs her pictures, how those pictures directly arrive from the point of view of the performer, standing on stage, seeing the crowd—but not seeing it really, rather feeling, sensing it. It is not so much the audience-as-model, but that what emanates from the audience becomes material for the paintings.

Yet, it is equally possible that the subjects are imaginary.

The watercolor faces might speak to me of soft dialectics, of sovereign subversion, unhingedness, and the possibilities of vulnerability within pose, armor, makeup, mask, joke.

They might speak to me in a kind of physically affecting way: how they illuminate themselves, the way when it rains with no end, water can go anywhere it wants to—a certain autonomy.

Yes. Most of all I like that they don't give a damn.

Recently, I spotted a large-scale picture book about the Scandinavian black- and death-metal scene on Kim and Thurston's kitchen table; it included a discussion about the scene's extreme specificity of aesthetics, general defiance, and total resistance toward most forms of regulated exchange with the rest of the world.

And it connected to another conversation in which Kim had spoken about her more abstract face paintings as having been partially inspired by the face-painted characters of black metal. In the book, attached as a kind of motto, was this Guy Debord quote, which I would like to re-quote, to form a last blotch on this page:

"There is nothing more natural than to consider everything as starting from oneself. Chosen as the center of the world; one finds oneself thus capable of condemning the world without wanting to hear its deceitful chatter."

– Jutta Koether

† Unless otherwise noted, all quotes from Jean-Luc Nancy, *The Ground of the Image (Perspectives in Continental Philosophy)*, (Bronx, NY: Fordham University Press, 2005).

Kim Gordon comes at language sideways. That may sound trite or quaint, but I do not mean to suggest that she has an especially marginal or idiosyncratic take on the written word, or speech. What I mean to convey is more literal: She has a distinctly physical response to language, and an interest in the lives of poets and writers, those beings who, for the most part, do not live in their bodies but, rather, the cave of the world and the self, searching for some kind of light, or reason. That is closer to the mark. I hardly knew her at all when, very kindly, she had me over for dinner one night. I was chatting with a member of her large, extended family, when Kim sidled up to me—there is no other word for it—and said, quietly, softly, how much she liked a piece I had just published, especially the form. I was struck by this—the visual artist's response to a piece of writing's formal qualities. I was also struck by how she got to the heart of what I had tried to do in the piece, all in an effort to subvert its faux empirical, journalistic "truth", to give it a form that resonates, possibly, outside the confines of a magazine. The truth is, very few writers can bear to see their work in print; you can't correct, or take back, what's been published. (Technically you can, but only in subsequent editions of a book. No magazine would run a retraction based on a writer's unhappiness with their style, or product in general.) Perhaps Kim came at me sideways that long ago evening to spare me the physical injury of a direct compliment. Writers always live with the sense that they've failed language. To thank them for their words can sometimes feel as though one is being clubbed with a prize one hasn't earned.

Still, art's a pleasure. Sometimes it's a shy-making one. So much to read! How will one ever measure up or write anything as glorious as what's come before? So much art to look at! How will one ever measure up to the task of trying to articulate what Kim Gordon has tried to do, and has done, in her singular work?

I come at Kim's paintings sideways because the freedom she exhibits in them makes me acutely aware of her physicality, a nakedness that always makes me turn away—at first. But once I've turned away from that feeling, I want to look at her work again and again. These feelings can come at you sideways. Being a contemporary painter, Kim is not separate from her work, in much the same way that Pollock wasn't separate from his "overall" approach, or the great Agnes Martin's piercing blue eyes weren't separate from the muted blue of her canvases, not to mention Warhol's desire to be seen and to see others as an extension of himself.

While I also look at Kim's paintings as further evidence of her willingness or desire to articulate the facts of her experience—what she sees and feels so acutely, so splendidly—and not, all at the same time. Her speech, suffused with pauses and directness, quiet reflection and a near novelistic sense of detail and memory for conversation, is the aural corollary to her visual work, which swims in the language and non-language of what she sees: girl heads, twilight, eyes looking at her as she performs, faces she and we half remember, as though recalled from a collective, half-forgotten dream, splotches of elegantly placed color that merge, somehow, with the colors in one's home, not to say one's head.

Despite the fabled coolness of Kim's various surfaces—both as visual artist, and performer—one is struck, again and again, by the depth of feeling behind her brushwork. She's a perennial youth discovering her material for the first time, always surprised by what it, and she, can do, which is to encompass and represent who we may be.

That last line is a partial quote from Shakespeare. Growing up, Kim's older brother loved Shakespeare and sonnets. There's a photograph of them taken in their youth. In it, one observes Kim's brother talking as she looks on, hearing and seeing him all at once. If everything is autobiography, might one say that Kim's visual art is an attempt to hold on to, and understand and show, the world that poets speak of, happy to let their words disappear once they've been spoken?

– Hilton Als, Northampton, 2008

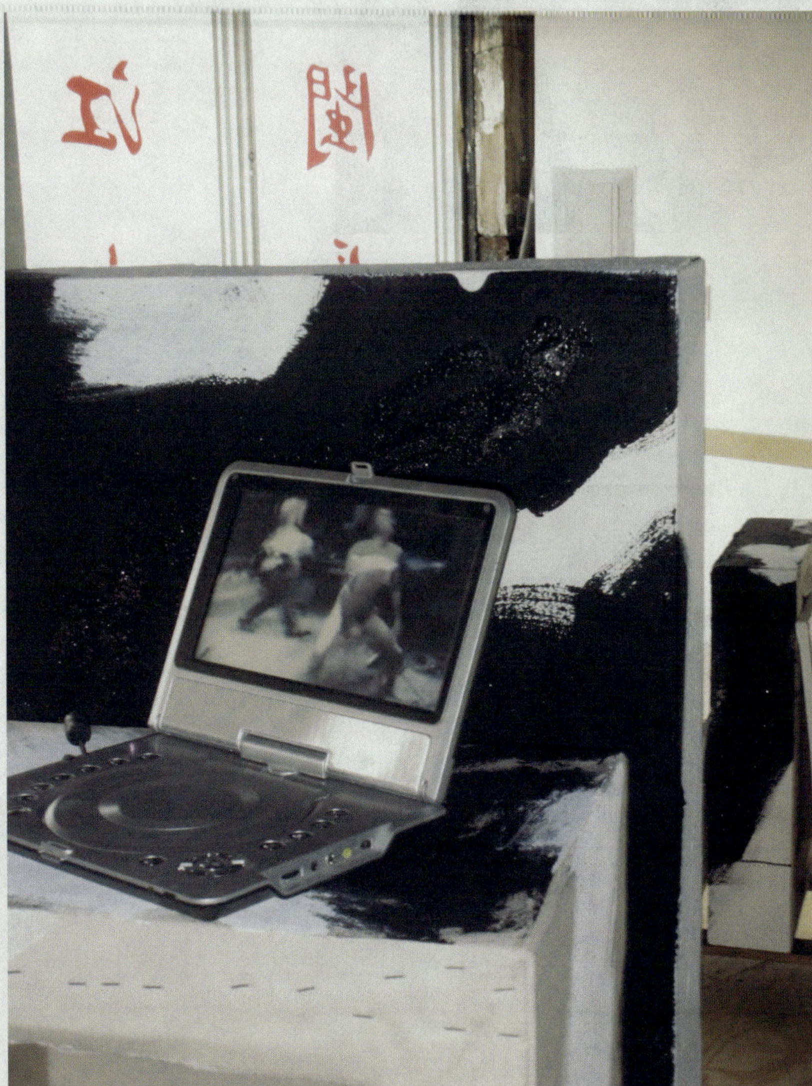

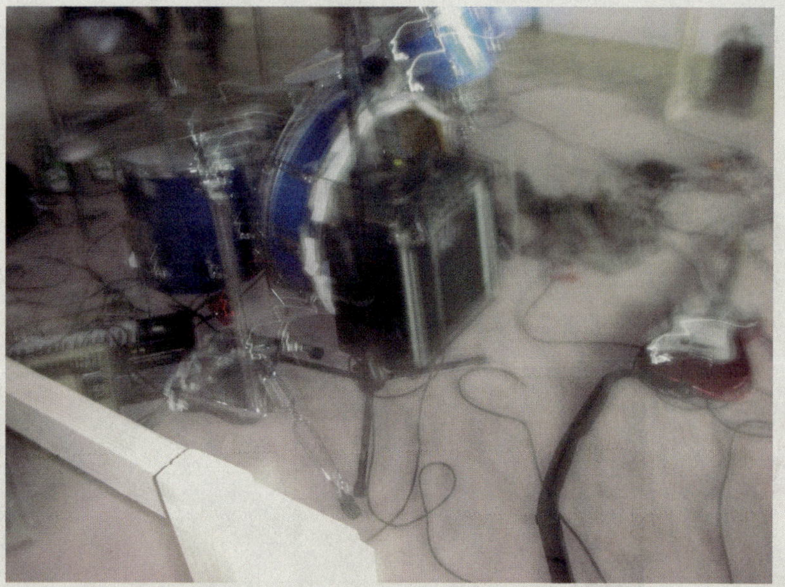

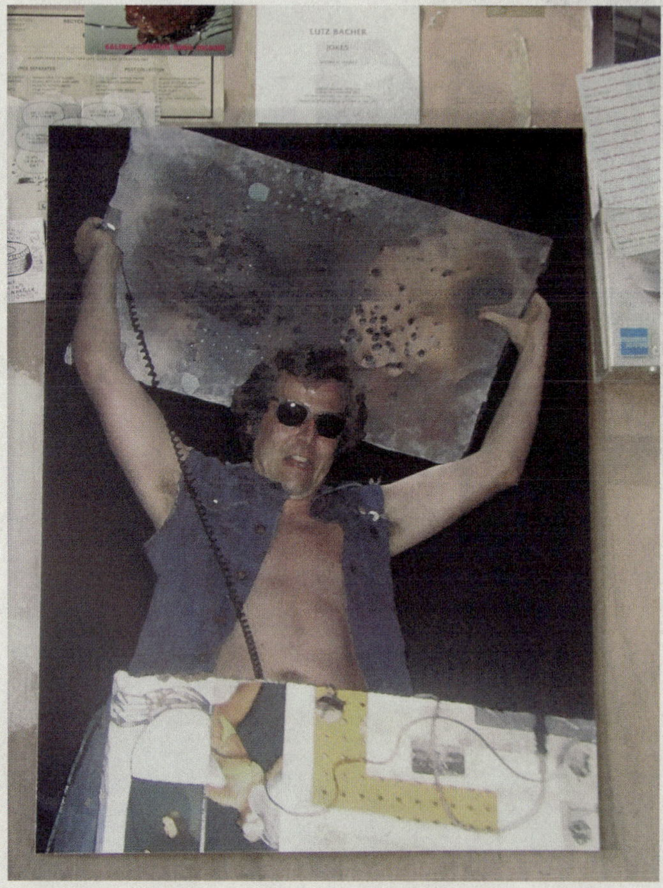
LUTZ BACHER
JOKES

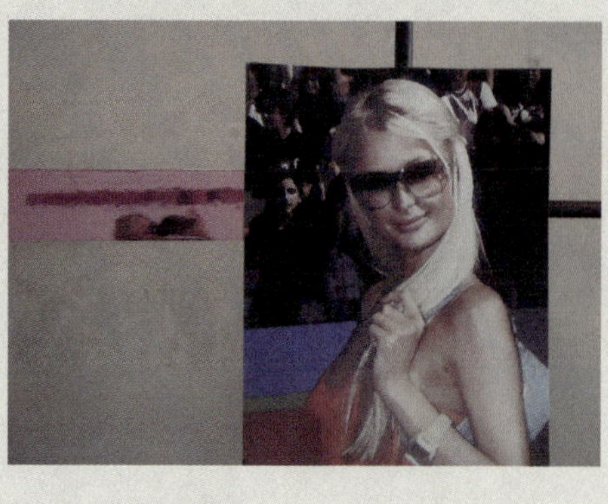

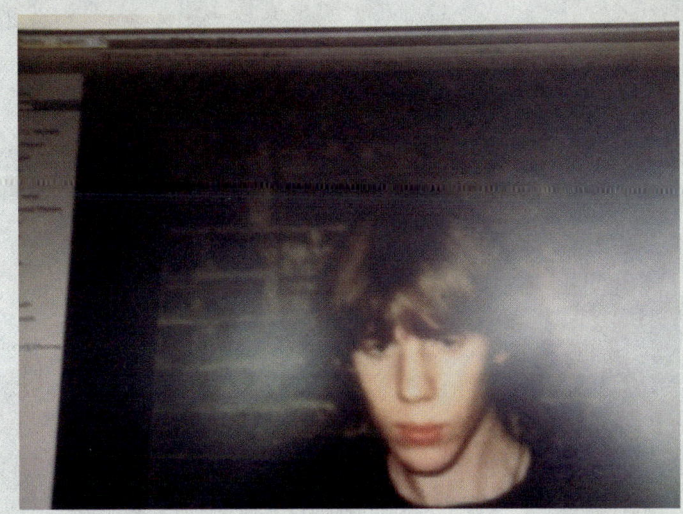

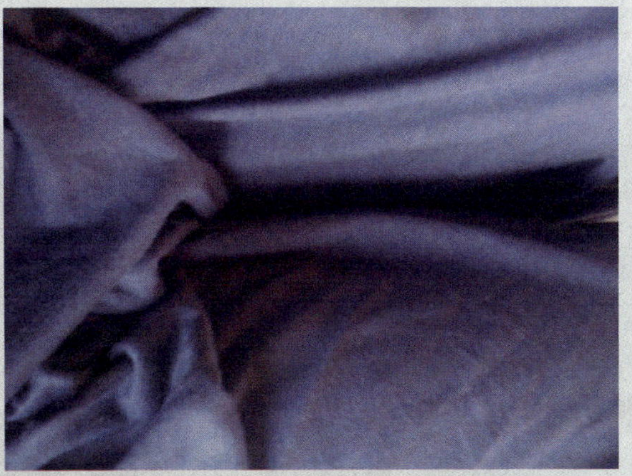

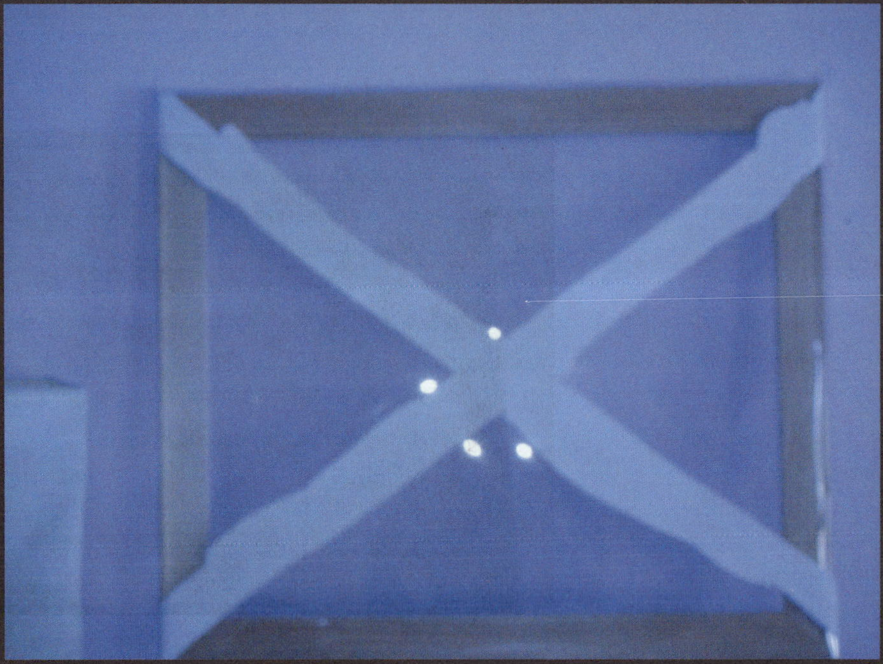

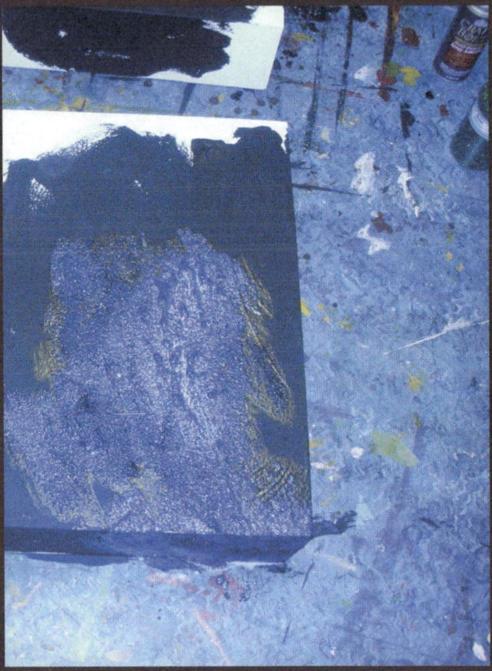

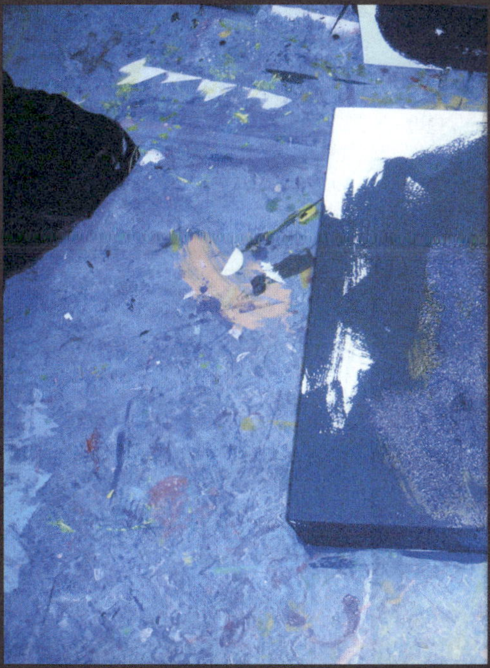

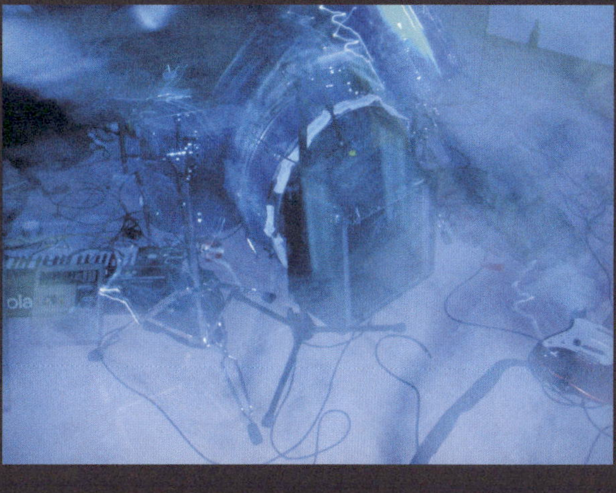

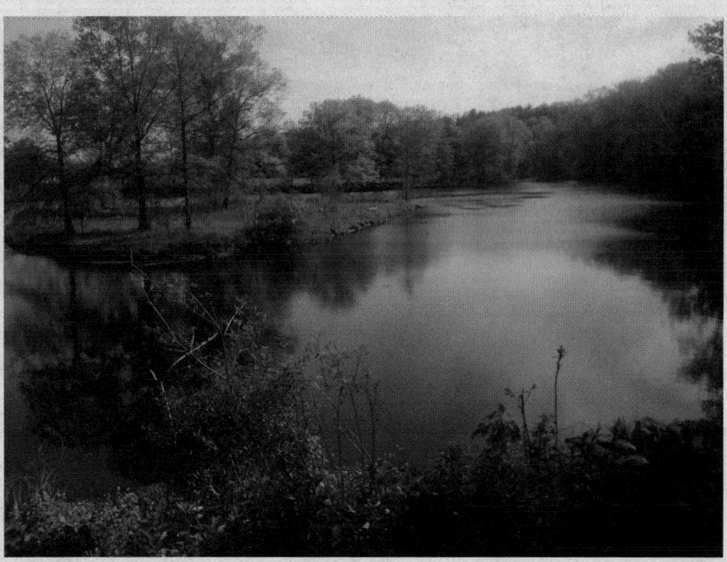

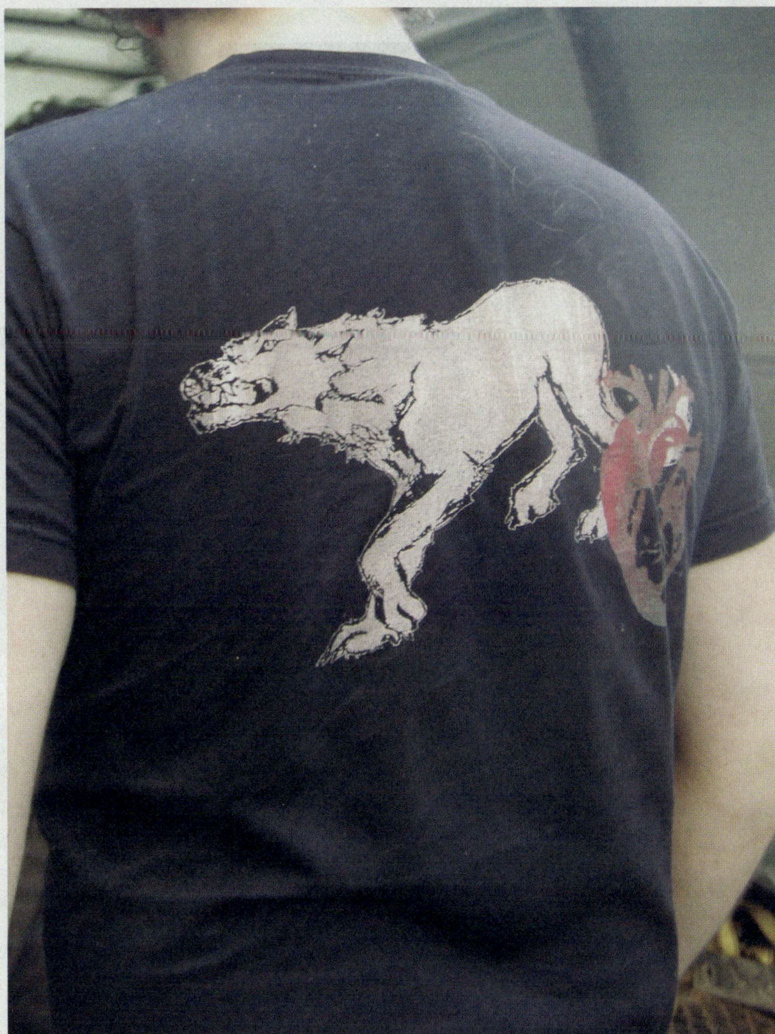

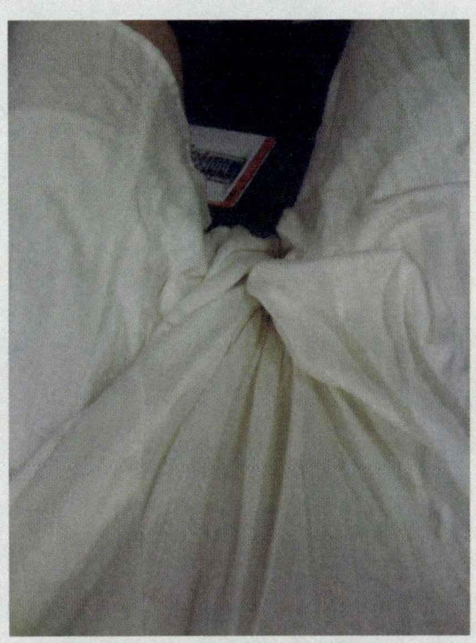

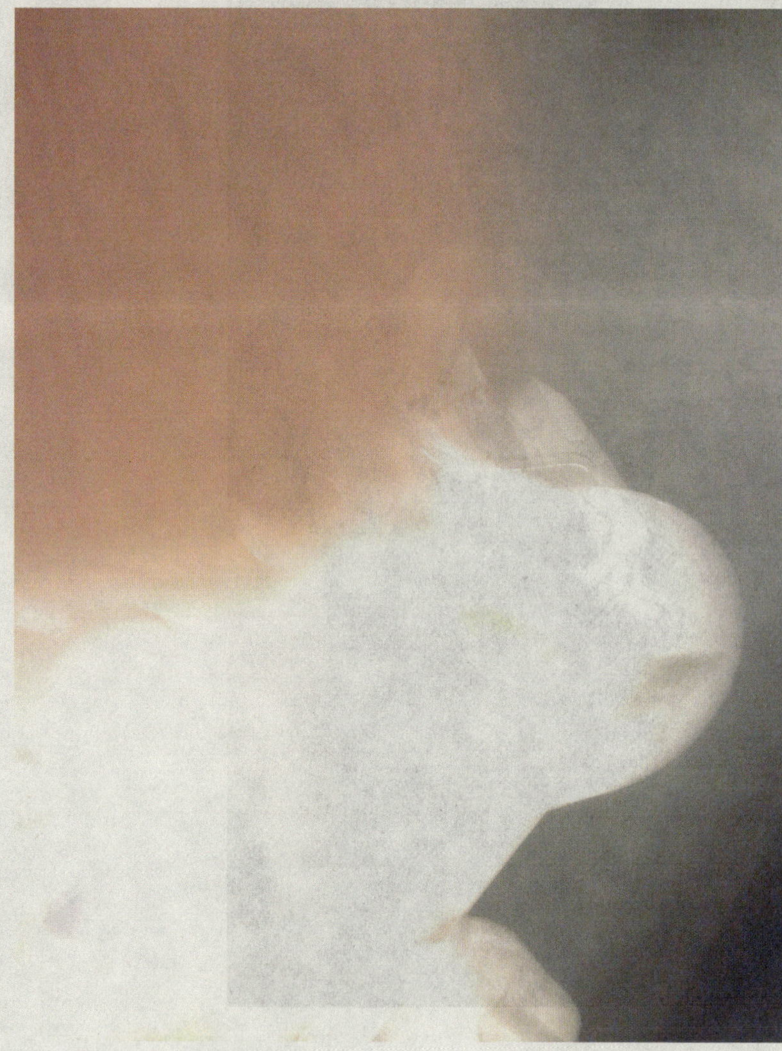

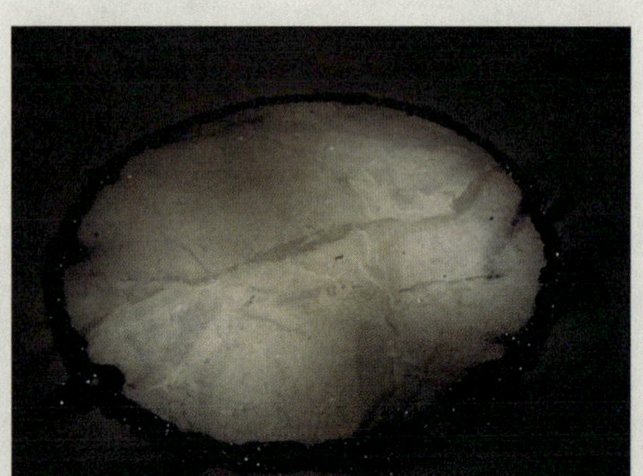

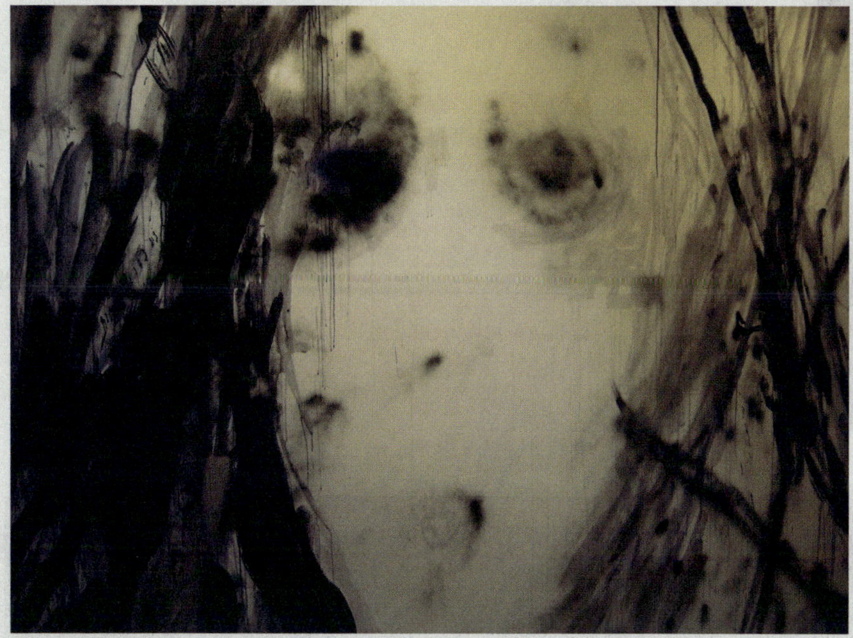

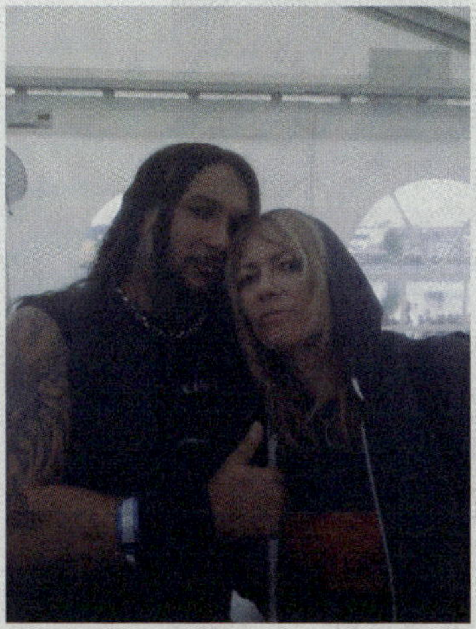

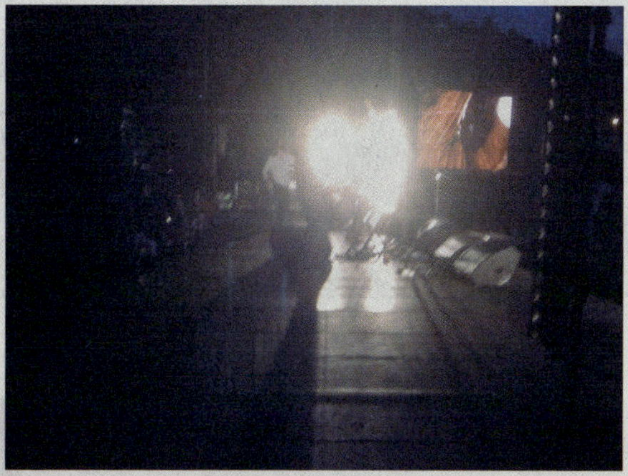

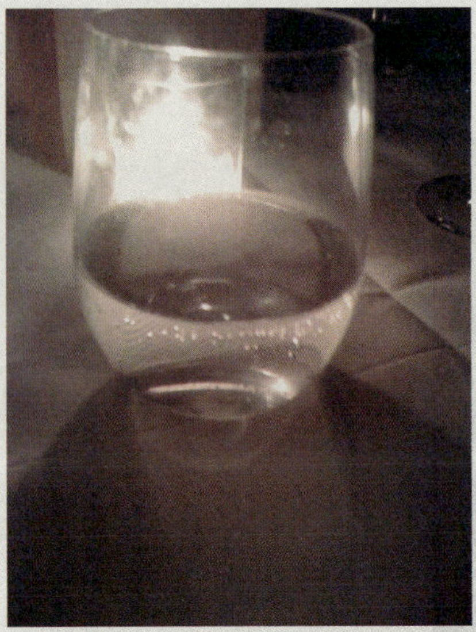
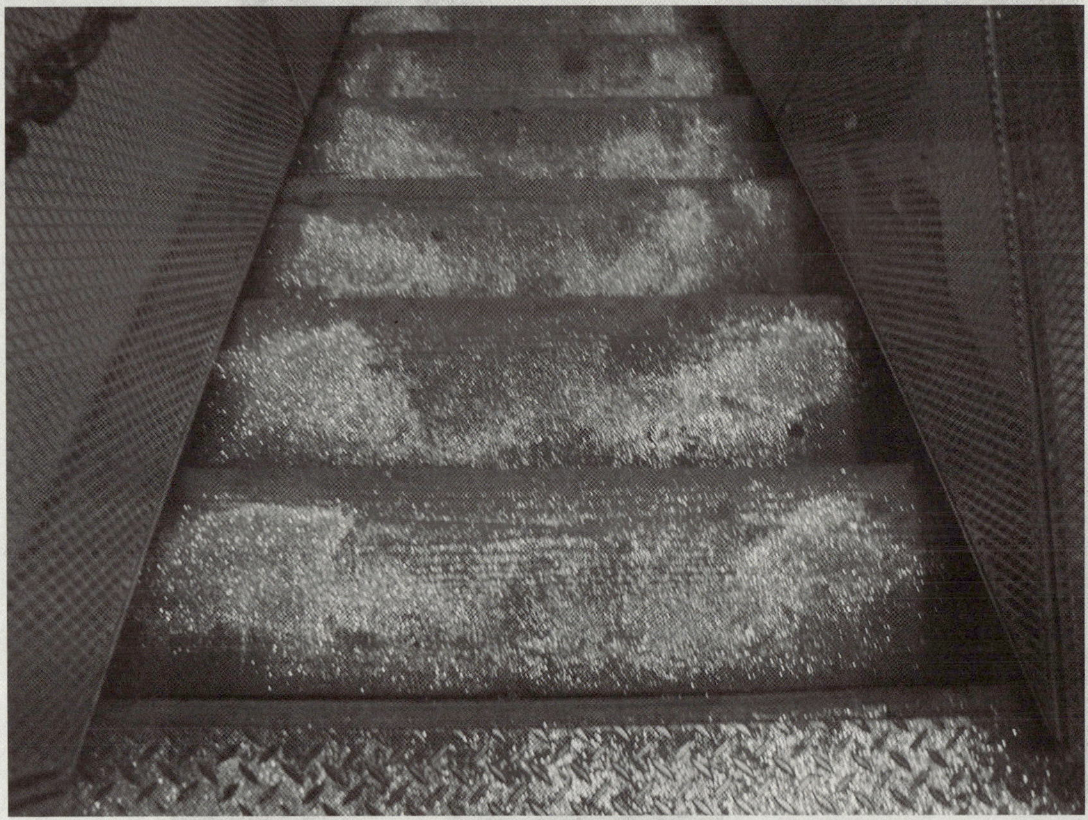
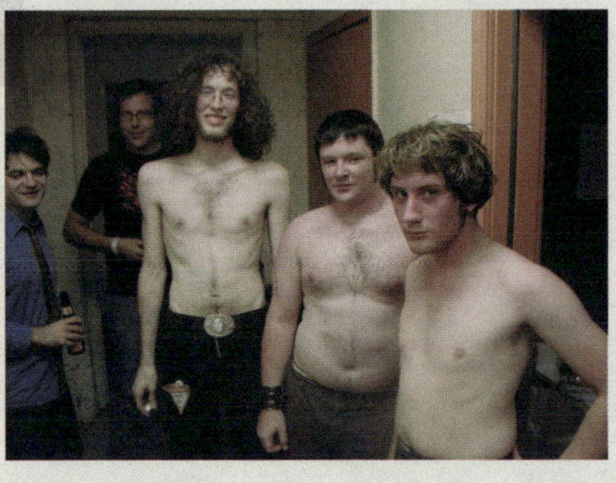

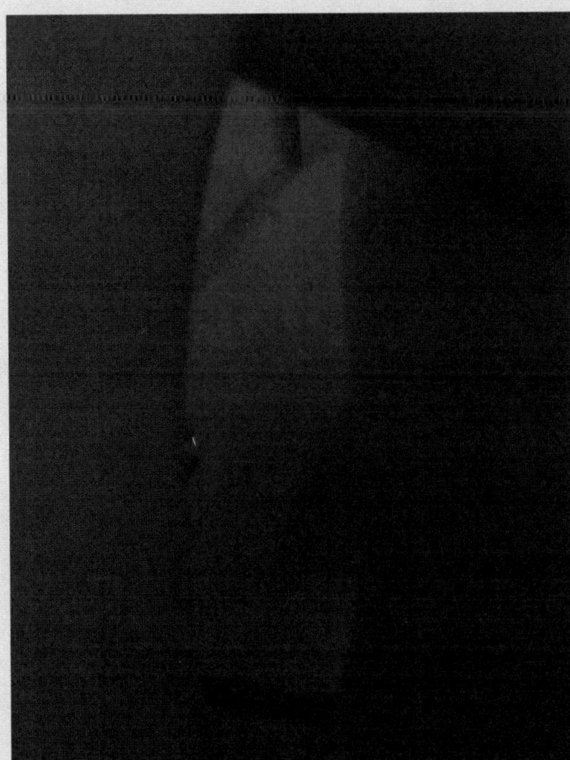

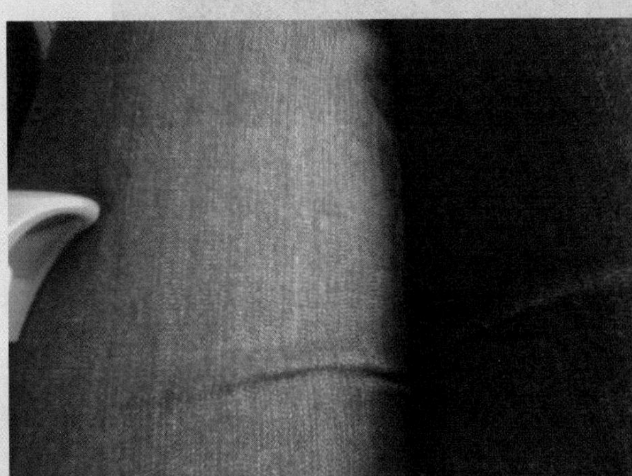

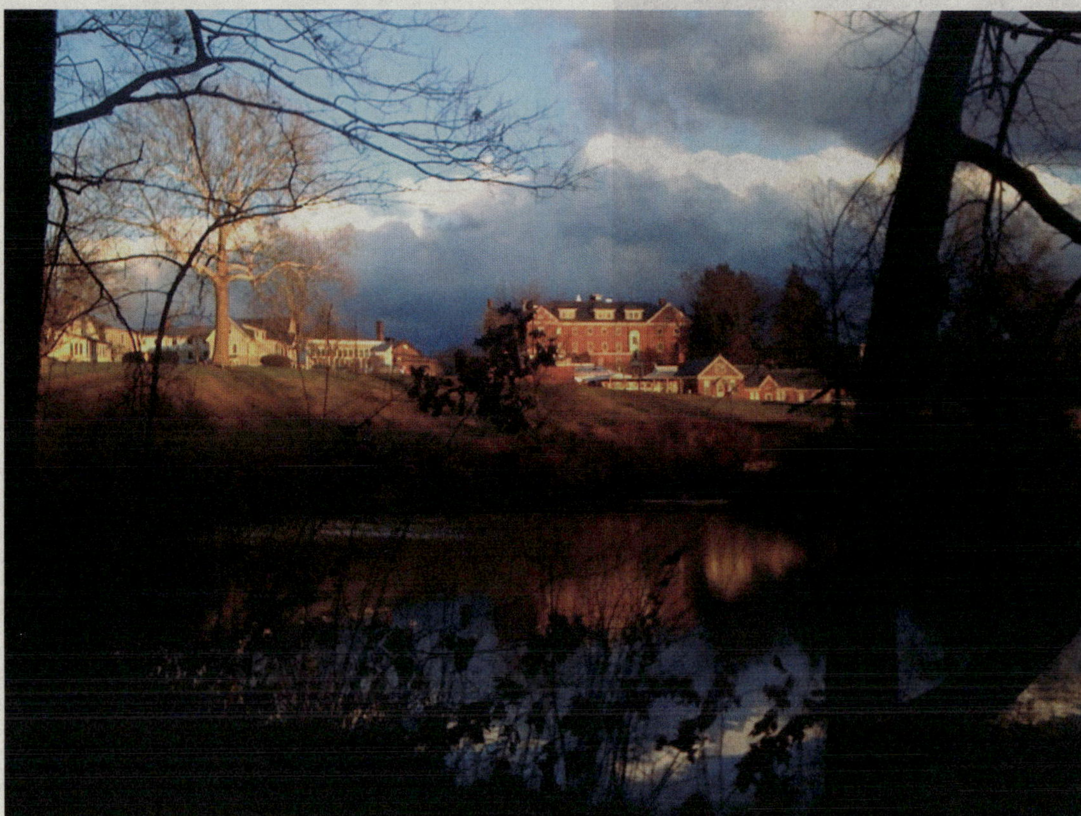

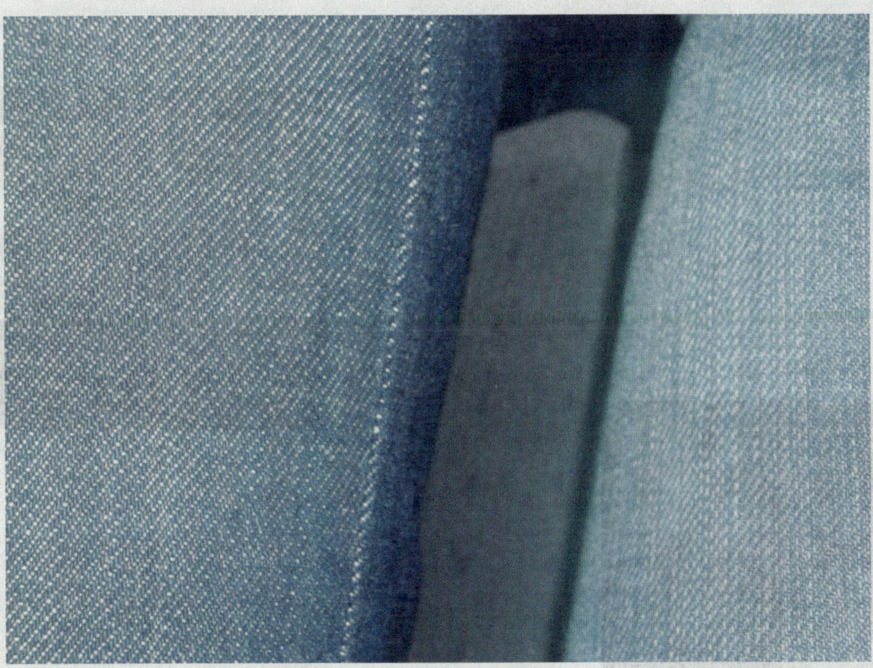

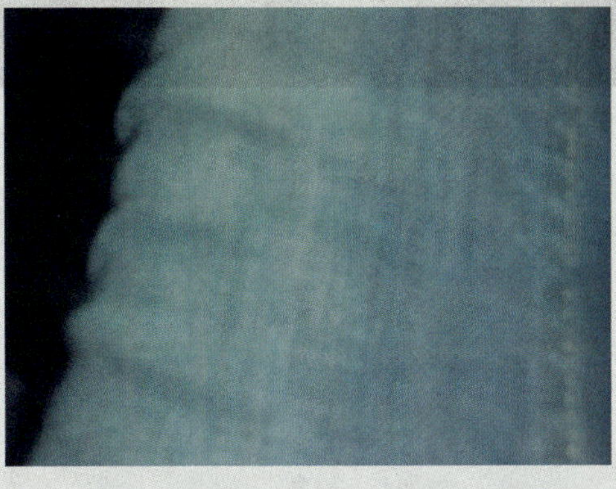

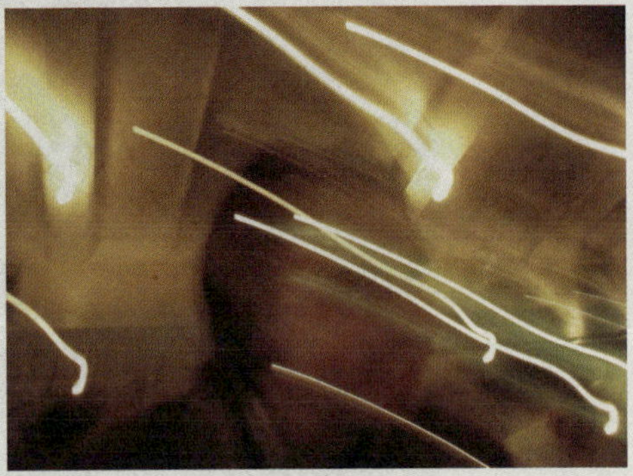
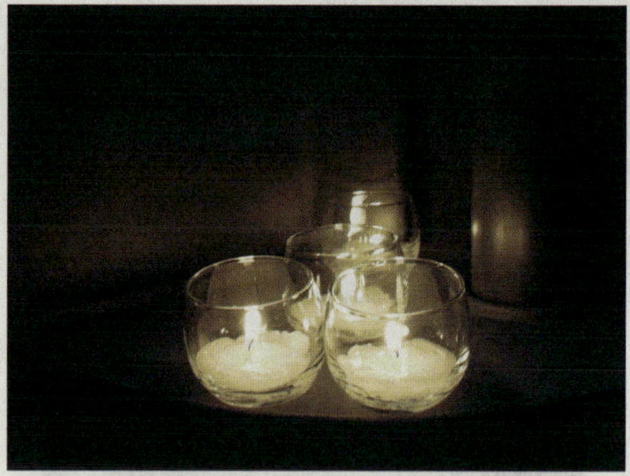
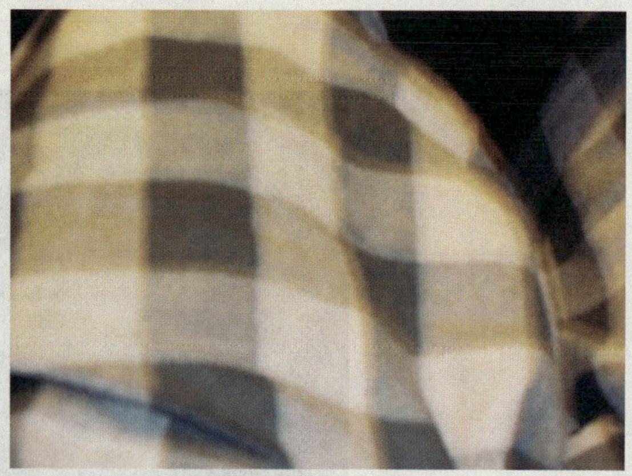
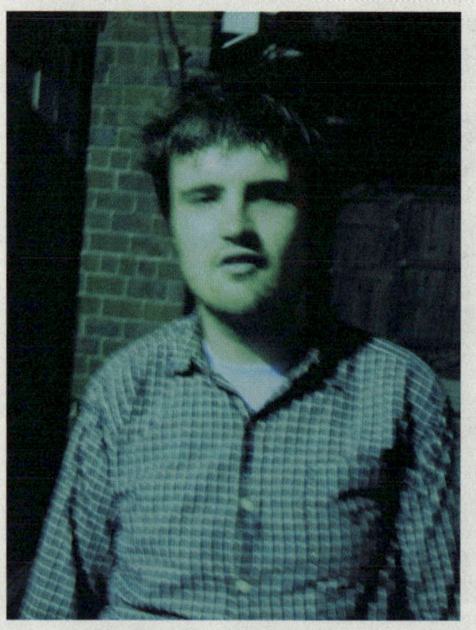

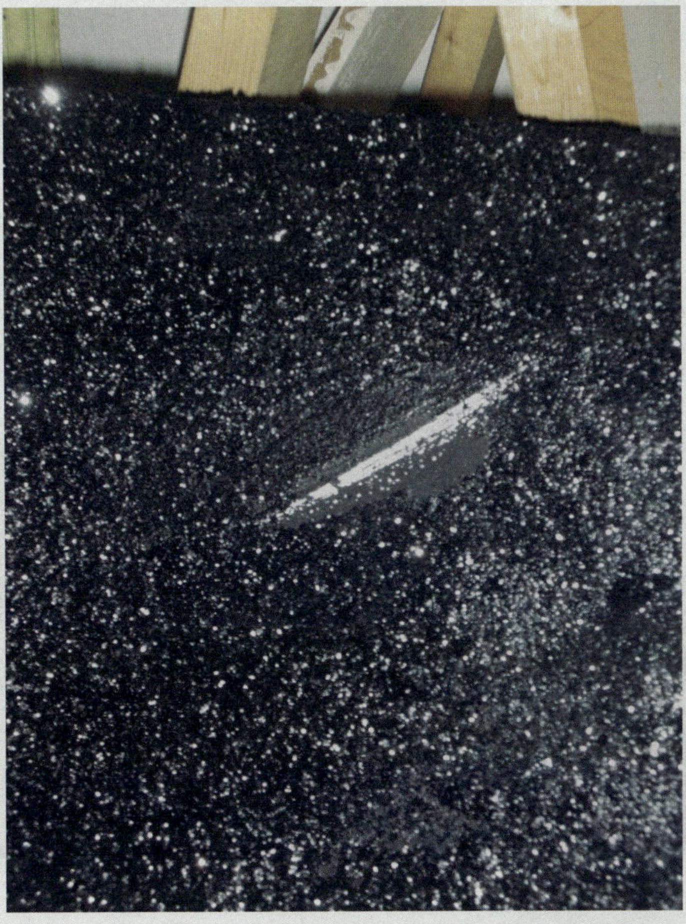

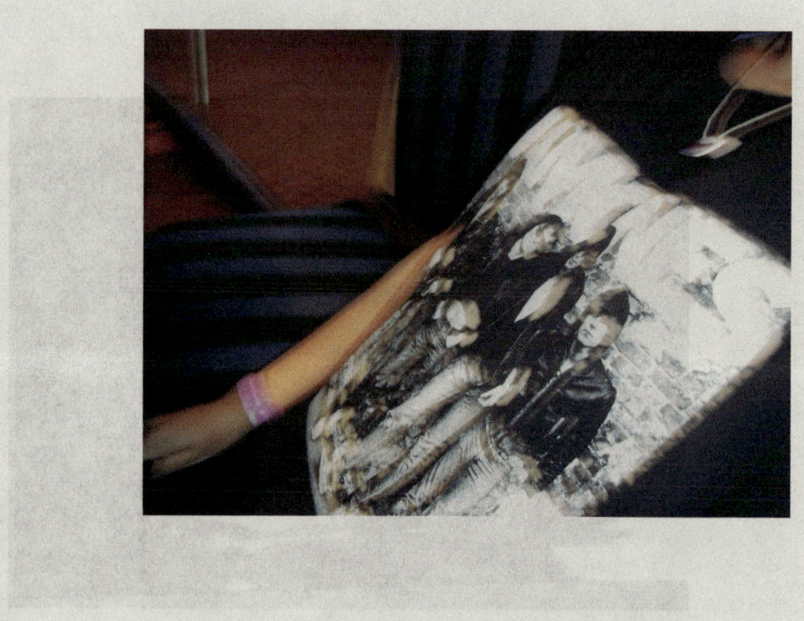

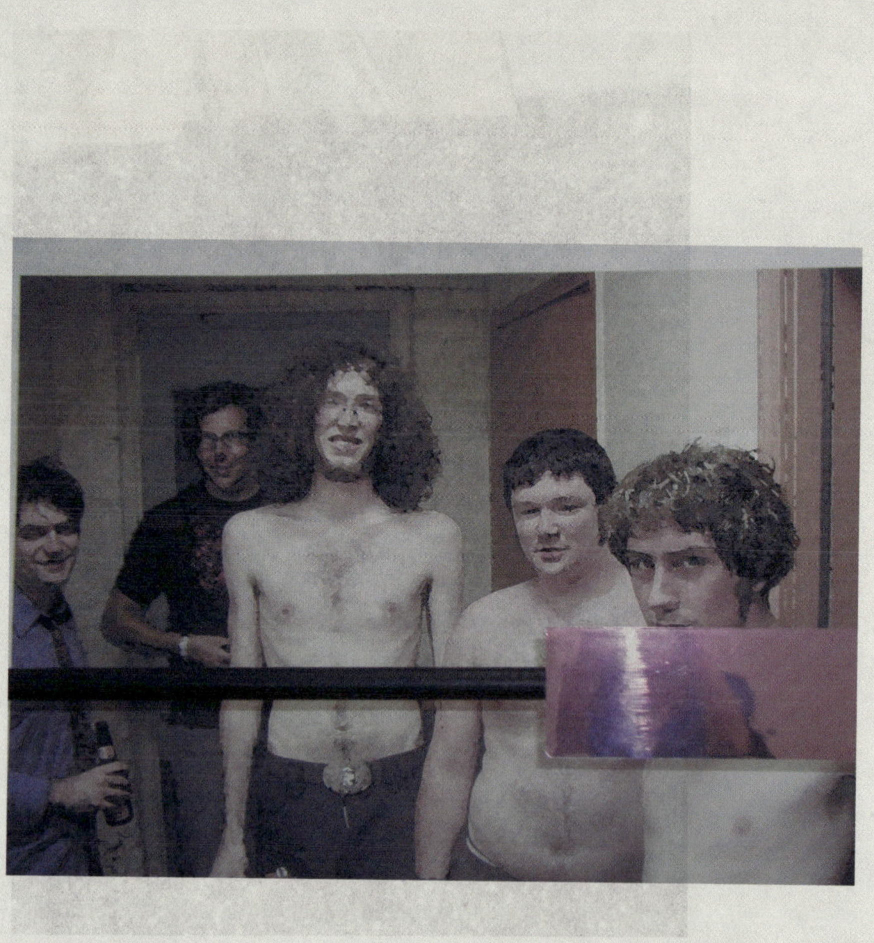

Feminine Frenchness nature lover lake poet dandyisms
Confusion via feminine his right to play feminism, female muteness
He rooted around in the bushes
he rooted around in the bushes
Turn to a tree, bird noise don't despair it's thorny here
she's afraid to put it on he's afraid to put it on
Girls on the run
Girls on the run, never fistfight, never fistfight
Common lips speak poet speak poet
Put it on put it on

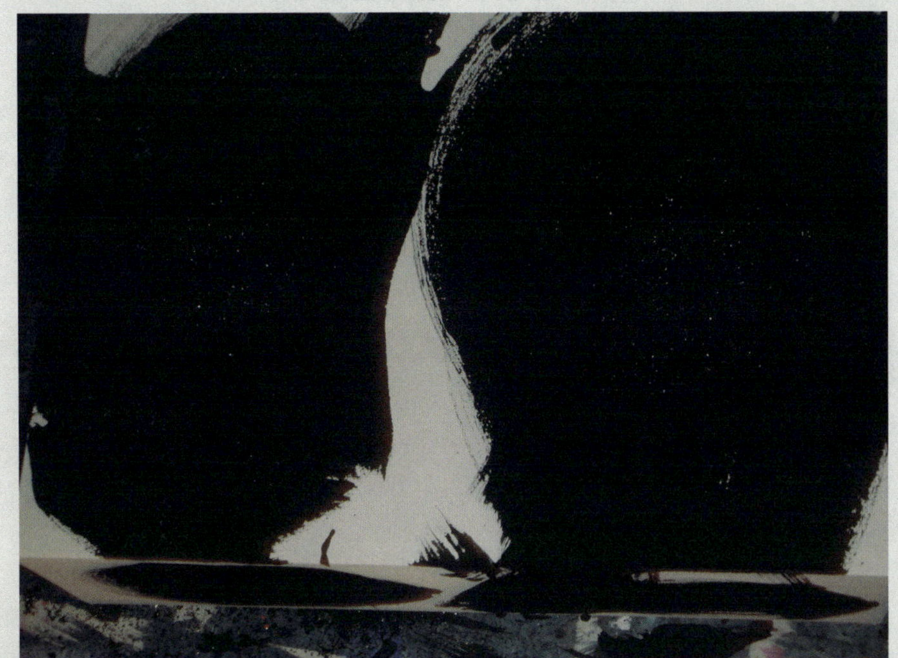

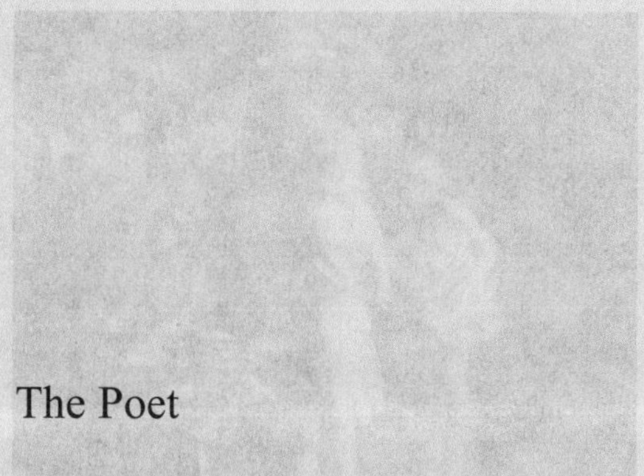

The Poet

Feminine Frenchness nature lover lake poet dandyism
Corruption via feminine his right to play feminism, female muteness
He routed around in the bushes,
he routed around in the bushes
Turn to a tree, bird noise don't despair it's thorny here
she's afraid to put it on he's afraid to put it on
Girls on the run
Girls on the run, never fistfight, never fistfight
Crimson lips speak poet speak poet
Put it on, put it on
Girls on the run
Girls on the run
The NY school ain't got chicks
The NY school is made of dicks
Girls on the run
The poets' trippin down, poets' trippin down.

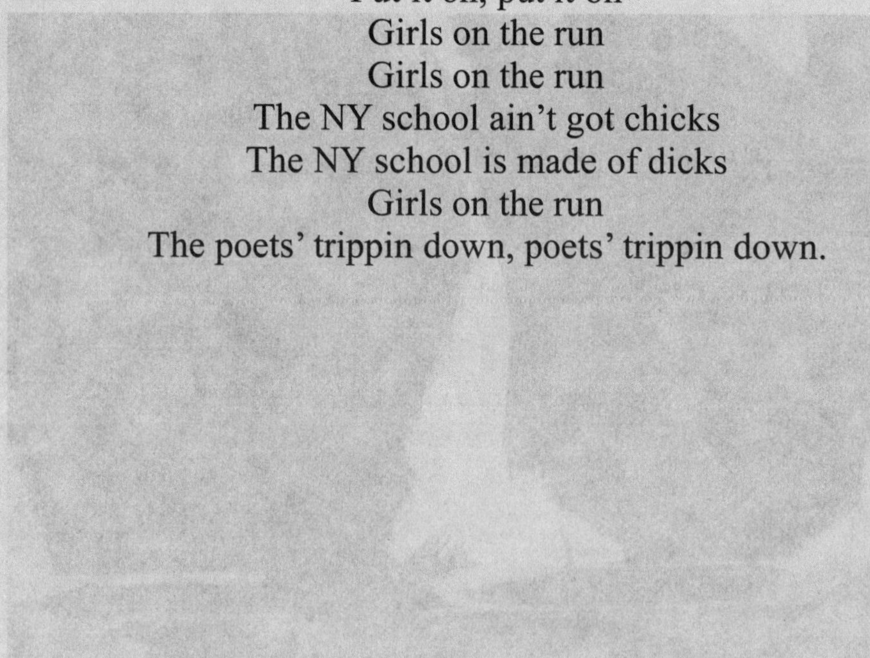

Monster Eyes

Monster eyes, monster eyes
Monster eyes, they follow you
Don't look too close
Monster eyes
The band was dreaming
Without you
You know i, just one secret
I won't tell if you won't tell
Just one … lost it
Come play
Be good to see
What's goin on with you
Without you
Good bye, good bye
Shudder to think,
To say goodbye

Surfs Up

Yr cold, yr hot, yr cold yr hot
Get inside, get inside me
You die and slip into a … ooh

You can lie in the summertime
You can die in the summertime
Yr cold yr hot
Get inside a heart of … what
You talk in circles, you talk in circles
Around me.
I long to touch you
I long to touch you hey
Go to work, surf’s up.
You can lie inside
You can die in the summertime
Yr hot, yr cold
Yr hot yr cold
Getting inside me

Free Kitten on the Mountain

A virtual eye,
Virtual lie
See you on the mountain,
Come on,
Come on
Let it sway, oh
Come on,
I'll race you to the top,
Go,
Does she cry, if yr heart goes round,
So steep, is my heart,
Turn it on push it, push a button,
And the campfire
And the wind on the mountain top
Don't rush it,
In the grass,
Rolling down,
Rolling down the mountain, catch me
With the shadow you can touch,
Crash, cotton touch you had me with the first look
Scratch, willow. Look in the distant thought,
and the pop star and the drugs, you crawl to me, touch.

Billboard

Look who's wearing the pants
Teenage lust
Skintight jeans they hug the curves in all the right places
A sexy spin,
Look who's wearing the pants